Just
Visiting

First published 2021

Text copyright © Michelle Bouverie 2021
The moral right of the author has been asserted

All rights reserved. No part of this publication may be reproduced, stored in a retrieval system, or transmitted in any form or by any means, electronic, mechanical, photocopying, recording or otherwise, without the prior written permission of the publisher and copyright holder.

A self published title
Designed and produced by Adala Publishing
www.adala.com.au

A catalogue record for this book is available from the National Library of Australia

ISBN 978-0-6487116-8-1 (Print)
ISBN 978-0-6487116-9-8 (eBook)

Just Visiting

MICHELLE BOUVERIE

A HEARTFELT AND INSPIRING JOURNEY
THROUGH A MOTHER'S GRIEF

ADALA
PUBLISHING

Bella's song

Mumma, I am the wind,
Dancing through the trees.
I am the soothing touch,
Of a warm summer's breeze.
I am the radiant sun,
Over majestic seas.
I am the rain,
Easing the torrid cracks of our Divine Mother's pain.
I am the moon, Mumma
With a promise that the sun will rise again.
Don't look for me
Just see,
I am the energy which nurtures the seed.
I am the beauty of colour held,
In every blossoming flower creed.
I am love, Mumma
Held in nature's morning song.
May the kiss of the morning dew,
Caress your naked skin.
My love is all around you,
And nestled deep within.
Feel the loving pulse of Nature,
Beat through your heart's song.
For within it, flying free,
Is where my spirit now belongs.

Vigil

THE SOUND OF the heart monitor beeped. Continuously. The symphony of such had held our attention many moments before this one. The loudest sound in the room, which somehow with each occasion, became a trusted friend letting us know that our daughter was breathing, her oxygen levels navigating between strong, depleted or somewhere in between. Yes, we had been held within this sound before, as we sat waiting for doctors to enter and leave Bella's hospital room with their wisdom guiding us through each visit we made, when she needed that extra care in hospital.

This visit to the hospital had felt similar in its necessity. Bella had seemed depleted that cold week in June of 2016. It was the week that I had Bella and her two sisters, Kai and Mahala with me, as part of their dad's and my shared care arrangement. It was icy cold that week, and we had mostly stayed home to keep warm, filling our nights with cuddles, singing and the usual routines that we followed through our week together. Over the weeks, even months before, we had noticed that Bella's weight was depleting, even though she was following her routine with eating and drinking her milk. We had had our usual visits to her paediatrician and neurologist leading up to that point.

Both professionals drew us into the reality that Bella's body was starting to give up on her.

Bella's genetic condition was the first of its kind ever registered in the world. Geneticists had carried out genetic tests in 2012, and because she was the only person with the condition of having 108 genes missing from her 19th chromosome, there was no telling how this would unfold for her, or for us. One of the 108 genes that was missing was the one that controls the nerves' message from the brain to the muscle. This messaging helps the muscle to form and stay working. The deletion causes a condition called Neuropathy. I had done some research into this condition when Bella was one year old, not completely understanding the impact of such a path. However, in April 2016, Bella's paediatrician broke down the details of this condition, and what was playing out before us, in the unique body of our littlest love. A slow, degenerative process was beginning to take place, where Bella was becoming weaker and weaker. The minimal muscles that she did have would impact her ability to breathe effectively, which would seriously affect the state of her lungs. On that visit to her paediatrician, in April of that year, she emphasised the importance of time and providing Bella with the best quality of life that we could, as her body was slowly beginning to deteriorate. This image was a difficult one to carry with us as we walked away from that consulting room, but we managed to nestle those words with love in our hearts as we felt gratitude for the wonderful care we had for our girl, and the love which bound our family, even though as her mum and dad, we lived in separate houses.

It was very cold that week. Icy cold, in fact. The two younger girls, Mahala and Bella, returned to their dad's house the Monday following, and although I had noticed the lethargy in Bella's form, I did all that we usually did in these moments. Kept her warm, monitored her temperature, held her and loved her. A hospital visit just didn't feel necessary given that we had been in this exact same position so many times before when monitoring the intricacies which ebbed and flowed with Bella's health.

Bella and Mahala returned to their dad's on that Monday following to spend the week with him, and Kai, my eldest, returned to her dad's for her usual week-on, week-off arrangement. Although Kai did not share the same dad as the other two, there was no break in the love that the four of us shared. Bound so completely by our love for each other.

I have dived into that moment a million times over. That moment I dropped Bella and Mahala home to their dad's. I have felt into my heart countless times. Did I do enough that week? Should I have taken her to the hospital sooner? These thoughts stayed with me through the years since that month of June in 2016. At first, they riddled my heart with mother's guilt and illusions that something more could have been done, but as a mother whose love for her children runs deeper than the reach of the universe, I know I loved and cared for her with the greatest immensity.

So, when I received that call on the Tuesday morning from Bella's nan saying that she was with Bella at Wollongong hospital because she had taken a turn for the worst on the Monday evening, her breathing had been laboured and her temperature peaking, my natural thoughts were that this would be a visit like every other. My mind painted the picture of us spending the next three days in hospital as we usually did, following our usual routine of taking shifts to stay with our girl, until she was well again. I would take the night shift. If I can pick a favourite time in a place where she was sick, this was it. It was my time to climb into her hospital bed with her, as I had done countless times before, and hold her, listening to her breathe. What a beautiful sound it was to hear her breathing, her head on my chest and her hand always in mine as she slept.

The first few days in the hospital unfolded just as they always did. The 'shifts' were always shared between me, Bella's dad

Scott, and her nan, Lyn. Bella's paediatrician would visit her room, and we would, in most cases, experience the shift change in nurses. Familiar faces left and new faces entered, all caring for our beautiful girl. I recall the last couple of days before Bella fell into a deep sleep. The last time her eyes would be open, looking into mine. I had managed to extract some beautiful smiles from her gorgeous face, as I sung her favourite song to her; 'Truly Scrumptious' from the movie *Chitty Chitty Bang Bang* is our song you see. The song that she would listen to so intently, smiling and cooing as she did with her subtly toned voice. No words needed, just love oozing from her entire being. I sat beside her hospital bed that day and sang to her. As the song ended, I held her hand and told her lovingly that she needed to get better so we could go home.

The next day, Bella fell asleep. A deep sleep. It was the 2nd of June, and the antibiotics had not been effective. Doctors decided to trial a different antibiotic on that day. The monitor tracked her oxygen saturation levels whilst beeping in its mono tone, which in these moments seemed to be shouting at us to look, to watch as those levels escalated and depleted.

Still, a day later, Bella had not opened her eyes. She slept. Deeply. Her breathing laboured. Her body fighting a battle in silence against the poison of pneumonia in her lungs. Infection holding her down against her sheets with her beautiful head tilted to one side. The top of the bed needed to be raised so gravity could assist the flow of saliva down her throat.

Bella's paediatrician entered her hospital room on the evening of the 3rd June. She held Scott and me in her caring gaze and suggested we consider an end-of-life plan for our Bel.

End-of-Life Plan.

End-of-Life Plan!

Somehow those words, although clear in direction, just did not sound real.

This was not how this situation usually went. Normally, we would be in hospital, the doctors would come, the antibiotics would take effect. Bella would be her beautiful and vibrant self as we left the hospital heading home, passing by the nurses' station, sharing our deepest thanks to those that cared for her.

This was not how this was meant to be. NO.

But it was.

There we were, with all that had come and gone in the past, all the pain and the laughter, and the sorrow of being parents to this special little girl; now we were being asked to play God with the final part of her physical journey. It was a difficult conversation, with lots of hard facts to swallow. Bella's paediatrician had shared with us that the same issues Bella was experiencing in this very moment would eventually be the cause of her death. Her lungs were getting weaker every time. Hard facts. Hard realities. To consider whether we wanted to, eventually, have a tube stuck down Bella's throat into her lungs when ventilation and nasal prongs no longer sufficed. To consider the scoliosis of her spine, which was consistently getting worse, even with the support of the body brace she had worn for the most part of her awake days. Knowing, eventually the severity of the scoliosis would impact her lungs and other internal organs. Such foresight, there was no resting place for this decision that we needed to make in this very moment. It seemed her body was writing the story for her soul, shutting down slowly. Yet within five days the unfolding of this moment seemed to emerge so suddenly.

We placed Bella on high flow oxygen with a humidifier, with doctors coming in to check the carbon dioxide levels in her blood. She remained in a deep sleep and looked somewhat peaceful, even during an imminent transition to the next realm, which seemed so unfair for the love in our hearts for our girl, but totally a path her soul was selecting all on her own. Although so much was taking place all around her in our physical reality, her soul seemed to have already chosen how the next few days would unfold. The high flow of oxygen bore no improvement in Bella's disposition, and so it was removed. An oxygen mask and a gentle flow of oxygen replaced it, in order to keep her comfortable and to gently hold her on her way.

By this time, my parents were making their way up through the night from Melbourne to Wollongong Hospital to be with our girl in her final days here on this earth. The hospital staff had at that stage moved us into the room at the very end of the long corridor in the children's ward. No-one said the word palliative care, but this all soon made sense. The space was large, with enough room for visitors and family, and space to navigate being by her side, in all our overwhelming emotions, as she embarked on the next part of her journey.

Bones

Don't fear these bones Mumma,
I am love
I am light.
Breathe Mumma,
Our journey has no end.
The light of a thousand rainbows
Exist beyond our plight.
Sing Mumma,
Melt those clouds I see casting shadows on your heart.
Don't shed a tear Mumma,
My eyes shine radiant light from before,
And until then.
I am here Mumma,
Though my temple withers in your sight.
Don't fear these bones Mumma,
I am love
I am light.

Last Breath

WE WAITED, PATIENTLY.

We sat in her hospital room at the end of the corridor, holding Bella in expansive love, waiting for her spirit to release from the confines of her broken body.

The days leading up to the last day that warmth would encompass her cells were difficult for us. The feeling of clutching to every spike in the beeping machine beside her, telling stories of her breathing patterns through each moment. She had many visitors. Beautiful souls arrived to pay her respect, to honour her with love and friendship. To kiss her forehead. To hold her hand. To sit with her for a while.

Nurses had returned to Bella's bedside to take a reading of the carbon dioxide levels of her body. The first reading that they received did not give a clear indication of the level of respiratory failure that Bella was experiencing, and the nurse looked over to me to ask if another reading should be taken. I agreed to the second reading, which would only confirm what we knew. Bella was dying.

I recall standing next to Bella's hospital bed with my face towards the two nurses at her side. The sunlight coming through the window, so bright in its position, yet such a contradiction to the darkness that encompassed that spacious room at the end of the corridor. As the interaction with Bella's nurses continued, I felt a presence at the hospital door and turned to find my beautiful friend Lisa's caring gaze. Lisa was a nurse and was working a shift in the hospital that day, on another floor and in another ward. She did not announce herself, but just held space in a caring corner to oversee, just for a moment, the care that our girl was receiving from her colleagues. Lisa is one of my heroes. A guiding light on this journey.

The dark day progressed, and we had as a family, sat around Bella's hospital bed as she lay, not having moved from the tilted-head position she had been in for the previous twelve hours. I had taken position at the foot of the bed, sitting cross legged and touching her beautiful feet intermittently, not wanting to crowd her. We sat, pouring our love into her, with tears shared between us all as we watched and waited for her moment of freedom. I recall as the light shone in through the hospital window that afternoon, the sound of an angel resonating in the voice of Mahala, as she broke into impromptu song. Her love releasing from her body through tune and harmony. The words holding her love for her sister and captivating us all in her strength. The most beautiful song we could ever hear. I held my breath at the painful explosion of beauty in that moment.

Our Bella continued to battle through that night. The nurses on duty had provided her with morphine to help her with the pain of breathing. The children's ward staff offered our family rooms in which to sleep close by. Her dad and I remained with her, balancing on the edge of strength, and love, and all the pain that is held in between, in knowing that she was going to die that night. We took turns in sleeping lightly, but to sleep would mean perhaps missing the most crucial moment in our journey with her. We slept, depending on one to wake the other should the end of her physical journey arrive.

There were pauses in her breathing. The pauses became longer, and we lay waiting with the sharp knife-edge of pain bearing deeper and deeper into our hearts with each lengthened pause. Then her strained breath would return, but only for a while, as the pauses became more frequent.

By this stage Scott and I were both on our knees, with the darkest night looming outside her window, each of us holding one of her beautiful, milky-skinned hands wrapped in love, yet cold in ours. Each of us claimed an ear on her beautiful little head, whispering our love to her. Whispers. The strongest whispers and most fluent words of love pouring into her, telling her she was safe to go and that we loved her. Telling her what a privilege it was to have loved her so deeply for the four and a half years she had been with us.

The final pause came. The longest of them all. We both waited for the return breath, as we looked for answers in her beautiful face. The longest pause of all, and no return of breath.

Our tears flowed.

She was free.

As the layers of the next moments unfolded, her final gift appeared before us. A smile on her peaceful face.

She was home.

Fortress

I'll build a fortress for you my Bel,
No end in sight, as I kiss you goodnight.
Our armour so strong,
Your body's impediments would find
Another place to belong.
I'd take it all from you my Bel,
My spine to bend and curve with your grace,
My stomach to burn, with a smile on my face.
I'd watch you run on the sand as my body lay still,
My eyes fixed on you, my legs no longer working,
As I watch in awe as yours feel the thrill
Of the freedom in a jump,
And the sand between your toes.
My tears would be tears of joy then my Bel,
As my body released you of your woes.
I'll keep my mind strong for you my Bel,
Although I may waiver between the dark and light,
You alone look so deep inside me my Bel,
You alone feel our fight.
I am always yours my Bel,
Our hearts beating as one.
I'll be the energy you lack my love,
You, my inspiration and me, your voice
We will write this song together my love
Always counting our blessings,

Even though this path was not your choice.
Stay bright sweet spirit, stay strong sweet soul
Together forever, whatever our gift of time may be.
My love will encase us, your light shining through
My blessing every day, is that I am here with you.

Shattered Hearts

BELLA'S SPIRIT LEFT her body at 4.14 am on 7th June 2016 in that spacious room at the end of that long corridor. Our families entered the room as we sat around her lifeless body. The smile she left us on her beautiful face, taken in also by the nurses who had cared for her, to reveal the beauty of her spirit even in this darkest moment of our hearts.

My mum and dad took turns in holding her body, her skin tone already expressing the colour of lifeless. A tone of yellow in her pores. Her 4-and-a-half-year-old body heavy. We cried. Scott's mum washed her beautiful body to prepare her for the next stage of her physical journey. The moments are joined together in my mind with gaps, which I feel I may have been holding my breath. I'm not sure. All I knew was that she was gone in that moment, and even though the depth of that pain in seeing and feeling her go was ever present, there was also a sense of relief for our girl, who had fought the greatest of battles from the moment she was conceived to that last breath she embodied. This was such a tug of war of emotion. Pushing and pulling, yet asking us to be brave as we stepped into this moment of her no longer being with us.

Bella's sisters returned to her room and loved her too. Cuddled her. Held her. They said their final goodbyes. How brave they were. How brave they are.

The sun rose that morning. What I would have given in that morning light for more time to sit with her and say the longest goodbye I could. But it was time for us to leave her in her hospital bed, dressed in her blue pyjamas, her little head resting on the hospital pillow with her bed now linear, no need for the elevation to help her saliva retreat down her throat. Yes, it was time to go, so the next part of her physical journey could begin.

We said our goodbyes and Scott and I drove back to my house together. We did not cry, but we spoke of the freedom she was now experiencing being released from her body which had encased her beautiful soul, holding her captive for so long.

The next few days felt robotic. Many flowers arrived at my door. They lined the passageway. So many beautiful colours. Friends brought food and gifts to express their sorrow and their love. Although those flowers were such a beautiful representation of love, they rustled the shattered shards of my heart even more, as I knew, they too, were going to die.

There were conversations. There was also silence as each human in my home was grasping for some sense in this significant loss we were navigating.

Members of my family had driven from Melbourne to be with us, and over the course of the next couple of nights we would sit around a warm fire, held in the cold June air. There was laughter and there were tears. I think that is the beauty of having those that love you around during your time of greatest need. Stories can be shared, and laughter can be had, even though your heart may no longer exist in its natural form in your chest.

One of those nights will stay in my mind forever as friends had arrived to join us in remembering. We were all sitting around the fire as the cold of winter still held the crispness in the air. Mahala, who was seven at the time, joined our circle and invited us all to hold hands, to share love and to just be together. Mahala's wisdom shone through in that moment, her soul so much older than her years. So that is exactly what we did; we all held hands and leaned into the love which held our circle, as we shared our words of love.

It was the day after Bella's death that Scott and I began to make the arrangements for our Bella's funeral. We soon decided that it was to be a celebration of her life, and the unconditional love which she gifted us for her entire life. The steps of finalising a funeral were systematic. The appointment was made, and the coffin was selected. The celebrant was chosen, and the day of her celebration was to be 11th June 2016, for all those who wished, to come and honour her with their love.

The week leading up to her celebration, my family had driven me to the shopping centre so I could pick a beautiful dress for Bella's special day. A blue and white satin dress with a rounded neckline was the perfect fit for her delicate body, and along with her special dress, some of her favourite items would be placed in her coffin with her. Bella loved to chew the ears of a soft handheld squishy rattle. She seemed to enjoy the sensation of the fabric of the ears against her gums. We went through many of these iconic items, and for many moments of her days, she would have the rattle firmly placed in her little hand with one of its ears in her mouth, as she chewed with certain delight on her face. This item, too, would make its way with Bella on her journey.

I had discussed with the funeral director how I would deliver Bella's dress and the special items to my baby. She gave me directions to the chapel where the mortuary was located. As I recalled the instructions of needing to walk down the driveway, past the chapel, I never completely anticipated the impact this delivery would have on my already shattered heart and fragmented mind.

I had driven alone to the mortuary and as instructed, I walked down the long driveway on the side of the chapel which was located on a busy main street in town. As I rounded the corner behind the chapel building, the mortuary assistant stood in the doorway to the mortuary. He was a broad-shouldered man with neat short hair and was dressed in his white mortuary attire. He was the only barrier between my shattered heart and Bella's lifeless one. I introduced myself and said that I had Bella's outfit and special items for her coffin. He looked at me knowing that all that was holding me together in that moment was the love in my heart for my girl, as I extended my arm towards him to hand over the special outfit he would be dressing my daughter in. He did not say too much yet his eyes were caring and assured me that he would take great care with my girl.

I have flashes of my thought process in that moment, like an old movie in black and white. Flashes of her once joyful, yet lifeless body cold on a mortuary table. The little hands which had exuded such warmth and love as they touched my face, now cold and lifeless. Her tiny fingertips now a match for the coldness of that table. I wondered if she was still smiling. I wanted to see her, but I was unable. So many thoughts ran through my mind as I considered the broad-shouldered man standing before me, who would be doing his 'job' when tending to my child.

Still numb, I returned to my car. I sat with my breath, the only support moving through my chest. I cried silent tears. I started the car and drove home.

The day of Bella's celebration arrived. Bella's story had captured many hearts, and the chapel was full of love. So many faces of so many people, yet there were moments I could not see anyone, except the beautiful pink and white small coffin her dad and I had selected, placed at the head of the chapel to be honoured.

The celebrant gave a beautiful service for our girl, and I cannot express how amazingly proud I felt of not only Scott, as he expressed his love for his daughter Bella, but also the pride I felt in the strength of Bella's sisters. Mahala and Kai chose to speak at Bella's celebration, and each stood at the microphone and expressed their love for Bella, bravely holding their words as they looked out into the crowd. I will never forget the strength they embodied in that moment. Both sharing the words which emanated from their hearts. Mahala at seven years old, had woken early the morning of Bella's celebration so that she could practice the speech that she had written. She practiced it a couple of times and then looked me straight in the eyes and said, 'Mum, I want to be able to not look at the paper most of the time when I am doing my speech.' She did exactly that.

My time approached to stand before the sea of faces present to honour my girl. I walked to the microphone with my gaze steady on the coffin, then slowly turned to face them. You don't ever imagine in your life that you would need to prepare a eulogy to express the love for your child at her funeral. Never had I imagined this would be part of my journey before falling pregnant with Bella. But life is funny like that. You just do not know what lies around the corner on your journey. You just do not know.

I could not cry. I wanted to be strong and make sure my words were articulated with clarity and respect for the love that had held her, loved her, and supported her. Most importantly, I wanted to honour her strength with mine in that moment. As I approached the end of the eulogy I had prepared in Bella's bed the night before, Mahala and Kai in a moment of impulse and care, came to stand beside me to hold me in their love. I am forever grateful for their strength and love in that moment.

At the end of the service we left the church first as Bella's favourite songs were played; one of them 'Truly Scrumptious'. We headed to the wake which was held at our local RSL. Food had been prepared by beautiful friends and family and so many people came to celebrate our beautiful Bella's life. We drank. We ate. We laughed. We cried. We shared stories. We came together for her and for the life she lived, for the battles she faced and for the ever-present energy of unconditional love which she vibrated so abundantly, even in the cage of a hurting body.

It was a beautiful celebration. A joyful one.

Community is so powerful in its reach and effect, especially when adversity or suffering breaches its shores and demands a pulling together of hearts, to support those in need. I have seen this beautiful display of humanity many times in my life and have experienced the deep healing which embodies such a coming together. Bella's funeral was one of those times. A coming together to support the breaking of our hearts, and to honour the impact our littlest love had on our community's experience in this life.

This same community had also supported our family in 2013 when I sought the help of a wonderful family friend, Lorraine, to organise a fundraising event for Bella and our family, to raise money for her care, and her many needs. Although these needs were not completely clear at the time as she was only coming onto two years old, I felt the pull to prepare for the journey ahead. The fundraiser was called Beats for Bella and after a huge amount of hard work, engagement with, and support from community, and an intense amount of organising, the event came together beautifully on the 31st August 2013. Local radio stations and the *Illawarra Mercury*, as well as online news platforms spread the word of our fundraising event and our Bella's story. A plethora of local and out-of-area businesses donated prizes to be raffled on the night. Three amazing local musical acts, Mikaela & Shelly May, The Hot Tea's and Chuparosa, donated their time to play some tunes at Bella's event. Music and happiness flowed through Scarborough Wombarra Bowling Club that special night of Bella's 2013 celebration.

We raised $6980 that night! An amazing coming together of community allowed us to reach an awesome goal. As part of that coming together, more than $2000 of the money raised was added to the $4760 I had raised for Northcott Disability through a separate fundraising online page, to honour the support the great organisation had given us by donating Bella's first wheelchair style pram.

Through this fundraising, myself and our family, as well as the special community which came together, were able to donate $7000 in total to Northcott Disability. An organisation which helps and supports many other people facing the same challenges as our Bella. What a beautiful extension of love and support, giving back through the power of a connected community! So beautiful in its reach and effect.

The money raised for our family provided support to us over the coming years. We purchased equipment and accessed these funds for everyday needs which arose. Eventually this special extension of community and support would allow us to provide Bella with a beautiful funeral and celebration of her life at the end of her physical journey with us.

Community was so ingrained in this journey from the beginning, and as we came together in joy on that beautiful night in 2013, we were held now in her death to celebrate the life she lived and the love and strength she shone so radiantly.

Our celebration of her life ended in the early hours of the morning, and I went to sleep afraid of what I would feel in the morning, knowing that the person I once was, was no longer alive inside me.

Dark

Its dark in here.
There's darkness everywhere.
I see flowers dying,
Their colour no blend
into my passage wall.
But it's still dark,
Their colour breeds no comfort at all.
Dark Night
Dark Day
Someone
Anyone
Please take my darkness away.
Pain has attached to the inside of my skin,
This skin, that I no longer
fit within!
Help
Me
"Help yourself"
Came the whispers from the shallow company.

Grief and all its Sorrows

THE NEXT FEW weeks unfolded slowly. My parents had to return to Melbourne. My daughters returned to their one week on and one week off arrangements with myself and their dads. Suddenly, my house was empty and the flowers that lined the passageway needed to be discarded as they were dying. I was home alone. I had not yet experienced one of those breakdowns you expect in the moments following the loss of your child. You know where you cannot catch a breath, and the screams leave your body without any control from your mind in their tone or expression. I was completely numb.

I recall standing in the room that Bella and Mahala shared and staring at her little bed with the Shrek and Donkey pillowcase that her little head had slept on only a few weeks before. The same spot where she would be hooked up to a CPAP machine which would sit in service next to her bed. The amazing device which had helped our girl so much as she suffered from severe sleep apnoea. She had undergone several sleep studies at Sydney Children's Hospital to monitor the impact this wonderful machine was having on her body and her breathing. The first test that was conducted to determine whether Bella was suffering from sleep apnoea revealed that she would stop breathing more than 20 times per minute! That was a scary result to hear, but over time that wonderful machine aided her so much in her sleep and breathing patterns. Some mornings I would go into her room, and she had obviously in the night rubbed her face with her little hand and the mask which usually blew the air into her nose, was situated to the left of her nose just below her little eye. Even though this mishap had occurred in the night, and could not have been very comfortable for her, she still beamed a smile so bright towards me as I entered her space.

I would turn the machine off before lifting the mask off her face and she would beam at me, with one hand at times reaching to my face, and we would just feel one another's energy. I would lift her into my arms, as she was unable to raise herself completely up, and had limited mobility. But I can tell you with the fullest of love and joy in my heart, that those cuddles in the mornings were the best. We were so happy to see each other and to start a new day together. Our routine so placed in time, and although no words were ever spoken from her gorgeous little mouth with her backward slanting little teeth, she spoke so loudly with her love.

The silence of our house screamed in that moment. I stood in the room she embodied so boldly, and began to feel the real deep gauges in my heart space. These deep gauges beckoning me to break, to cry and fall to the floor, to lay with the shattered pieces of my heart which seemed to be everywhere my eyes were placed.

The emptiness in the house was too great. I contemplated how I could live here with all this pain. The words looping around my shattered mind were telling me that I could not live here anymore. As we now stumbled through this new physical reality of Bella no longer with us, healing in our home felt obstructed by what I could see, and that was an emptiness too overwhelmed by memories. As I reflect now, I understand the desperate need to escape the pain, because it was all encompassing. So, I made the decision to hand in our notice, and find somewhere else to live and to heal.

Although it does not seem very practical from a spiritual sense to move house in the throes of grief, and after such a significant loss, my mindset was not able to sit completely with the discomfort of the feelings in my body. The confusion inside myself was a call to action, to keep moving somehow. To escape, where I could, the bold and intrusive feelings of nothingness and everything-ness.

My lease was coming to an end, and a cute and comfortable townhouse became available which we were approved for. My folks headed back from Melbourne in July to help us move. My parents are the moving wizards, and having their help was immense. It was the biggest gift they could have given me at that time.

Moving from a three-bedroom house into a two-bedroom townhouse was a mammoth task in my mind. Numbly walking around our home looking to start the packing process, from somewhere in the space. The major block awaited me in Bella and Mahala's room, where all of Bella's toys, clothes, equipment and many other trinkets were held. There were fleeting and consistent thoughts in my mind that I was betraying her by not taking all her belongings with us because GODDAMMIT, she had only been gone a short time! My mind was unable to really adjust to the thought that I would need to let go already of so many of her belongings, even though this call to action was my own choice, my own doing and felt necessary. The releasing of some of these items was necessary, but why was her death necessary! I would find myself in that loop of thought over and over as I walked in circles for countless hours over many days.

Eventually, and because it was totally necessary as the lease end-date loomed, I began to sort through Mahala and Bella's room. Bella's clothes were donated to the Salvation Army so another beautiful little girl could wear her pretty clothing, and in the fantasy of my thought process, perhaps feel her love somehow from the fabric that had once caressed her skin. I did the same with most of her toys, taking a few of her special teddies with us to our new home, but the majority went on to live in another's home, somewhere we would never know.

The special wheelchair-style pram, feeding chair and other equipment we had received through foundations such as ADHC and Northcott Disability were returned, for another little person just like our Bella to be supported in. It is interesting how when you are watching these items leave your home, you remember how they came to be there. You remember the amazing Occupational Therapists and Physiotherapists, Doctors and Nurses that all helped with filling out forms for funding and measuring and testing, and the time it took for our family to receive these golden objects of support for our girl. So much depth of experience and moments involved in their procurement. How lucky I felt to live in a country which supports the less abled in such a wholesome and refined way. We were also blessed to have the same physiotherapist, Lyn, for the entirety of Bella's life. She had started coming to our home to work with Bella in the first couple of months of her life and would alternate her visits between mine and the children's dad's place to fit in with our living arrangements. She had the loudest joy in her voice when Bella made those small, golden wins, and Bella would beam with happiness at her joy. Lyn was a wonderful light in our experience.

Eventually, our move was complete, and we were in our new home. Exhausted by not only the physical aspects of such a move, but also by the emotional pulling and feelings attached to such a break-away from a place which had been so monumental in our experience so far. The house we had moved from and where Bella's last healthy days were spent, had also been a monumental step for us as a family, and the one before that was monumental too. You see, when you have a child with special needs, and you are not a homeowner, there are many decisions to be made based on each level of development your child has reached. Many decisions, which will in turn, determine how that experience for your child with special needs will evolve.

Bella was five months old when Scott and I separated. I had rented a townhouse close to the ocean, in a nice complex of about eight townhouses. It had three bedrooms so the older girls had their own rooms, and Bella and I were roomies, with her in the bed I used to sleep in when I was a little girl. A comfy family heirloom with fold up sides so there was no rolling out. Bella's developmental delay meant that she was not reaching those milestones that she should have been at five months old, but here we were in our own little place, capturing the milestones she did reach when they occurred.

I remember her sitting on her own for almost a minute in the lounge room of our new rental by the sea. We were cheering her on and celebrating and she just beamed a smile, loving the praise and joy. One night just before sleep time, she grinned and with a determination in her face I had only seen a few times before, she pulled herself up from a laying down position to a seated position. This may not sound like much, but let me tell you, this moment was golden and filled my heart with hope that our girl was going to continue to get stronger and begin to reach those milestones eventually. I cried as she just powered through, doing it twice more, loving how expressive I was with my excitement and my happy tears. She thrived on positive energy. Absolutely thrived!

Six months passed in that first townhouse and we were happy living there. During the quiet times, when my girls weren't looking, my heart was grieving a life I knew my youngest daughter would not live, as I watched Kai and Mahala thrive in so many other ways. But this is the path you choose as a parent. To honour the steps they take, no matter how slow. It was here in 2012, that the diagnosis of Bella having 108 genes missing from her 19th chromosome came through to us. All language that I did not completely understand the impact or severity of. Knowing that she was the only person in the world with this condition did create more anxiety in my body. I tried to hold onto those moments of hope, where sitting for a minute on her own, reflected promise. A promise that perhaps the diagnosis would not determine her fate.

There were many adjustments to make as our family of four, moved from our family home where there was love of a mother and father, to now living separately and settling into one-week-off and one-week-on arrangements; we mustered through. My children are very resilient beings and through each stage of our process on this journey, they have expressed their strength and bravery so eloquently. I'm extremely proud of them for that.

Our first six months in our townhouse unfolded as best it could for us. Bella at almost one year old had not reached those milestones she should have by this stage. There was no sitting for prolonged periods of time, or attempts to crawl forward either on her belly or her hands and knees. By now both my other girls were either crawling and almost walking, but Bella was still needing to be carried, and placed comfortably where she would be seated or laying. Carrying her was never a burden, but I did feel that she was heavier at this stage of her development, than the other two had been. That perception derived perhaps from her inability to hold her own weight entirely, and feeling also into the bearing it placed on my own body. Still, to keep her close to my heart and to hold her as she held me with such a gentle touch, this was one of my most favourite gifts to give her. There was so much trust in her closeness and her love was felt heart to heart as we navigated from one location to the next.

Our routine was very much the same every morning. I would hear Bella wake and I'd bring her over to my bed for a cuddle and a bottle of milk. I would sing to her, and she would make those beautiful little sounds to express her contentment. We were attuned to the sounds she made. Some were happy, expressing joy, and others were indicators of her unhappiness, or of her discomfort and need to be moved. After our morning ritual, we would emerge from the bedroom and descend the stairs to begin the day. We would usually have breakfast and a play with her special toys we had received through funding platforms that provided toys for children with special needs.

It was a warm Saturday morning, and Bella and I had followed our usual routine before descending the stairs to the bottom level of our townhouse. There were two levels to the stairs. Five or six steps down from the top level, then a couple which turned the corner, and about six steps down to the bottom level. I had lifted Bella that morning as I always did, pulling her in close to my chest, with the inner elbow joint of my right arm supporting her bottom along with my right forearm and hand equally supporting her back. I had done this so many times before and being aware of her weight, I would wrap my left arm around her too, with my hand supporting her upper back where her neck began. I walked slowly down the first section of steps, her smooth forehead touching both my forehead and my lips intermittently and gently as we descended and took the turn for the final steps to reach the bottom level. The stairs were an extension of the fake floating floorboards which lined the bottom level floor.

One step, two steps and although I cannot grasp how or what impediment resulted in such, I placed my left foot down too close to the edge of the next step; the ball of my foot slipping off and my left leg extending down along the steps. As I tried to overcorrect this action, my right knee bent and came down to the steps, with my arms clutching, but gravity pulling us both forward. In slow motion I felt and watched as Bella's weight reached forward too and she slipped up, over, and out of my arms. We both fell forward, my arms reaching for her as I watched the fear from her eyes pierce into mine. I threw myself forward with all my might to try and at least catch her before she hit the floor. The sounds that came bellowing from my mouth would have scared her more as I heard the heavy thud of her connecting with the floor, followed by the muted shrills of her pain coming from her mouth. My own screams deafening in their resonance as I landed next to her on the ground, wailing.

Her screams only sharp, muted shrills but deafening all the same, and mine so loud as I felt the deep failure as a mother for not being able to keep her safe or catch her in that moment. All sense did try to intervene that the heaviness of her body gained momentum past my ability to save her and the obscurity of how my legs were placed in their dysfunction, but the sound of the 'thud' as she connected with the floor shamed that sense right out of those next moments. I pulled her into my arms, rocking back and forth, checking her for signs of more damage than her poor little body had already suffered in her life. 'I'm so sorry my Bel, I'm so sorry', is all I could continue to cry and wail, as she whimpered in my neck. I'll never forget the whimpering, and the silent cries which she expressed.

My neighbour entered my house as my screams must have reached the water's edge for they were so full of sorrow. 'We fell down the stairs, we fell down the stairs!' is all I could shout from my heart to her. 'We fell down the stairs, I couldn't get to her, I'm so sorry'. My neighbour remained calm as she pulled us both up from the floor, Bella and I still locked in the embrace which I was not prepared to let go of. She managed to get us over to the lounge and called a doctor who lived in the complex too. I called Scott crying into the phone that I had fallen down the stairs with Bella. He came over too.

The doctor arrived within ten minutes and checked Bella, who by this stage was smiling and sending her love into my eyes, perhaps her way of comforting me. All I could do was say sorry to her, to ask her to forgive me.

The trauma of that moment stayed, and the very next day I rang our real estate and explained the situation that the stairs were not safe any longer as Bella was getting too big and heavy. I needed to break my lease and move into something that was flat.

Monumental moments seemed to be a driving force for our moving. I found us a beautiful house close to the water. More money every week, but it was a single storey, with enough space for myself and my children and for Bella to explore in with her new walker which was due to arrive soon. We did love the space and the yard of our new flat home.

The scars left by those stairs have remained in my heart, although they have softened with the forgiveness I had to give myself as sense made sure I understood that although I was carrying my child, and taking care, circumstance in that moment brought it to what it was. An accident. A lesson. A push to move. A need for change. So, I listened. Fast forward two years, and here we were. Moving once again. Another monumental moment, but this time my Bella's passing was the monumental moment which if I could, I would have replaced with any other. I could not keep us in that lovely flat house which had provided her with so much more room to be. Just to be. To explore walking backwards in her walker, as that was the only way she knew to do it. We tried many times to help her progress forward with her special little feet in that walker, but backwards was better for her at that stage in her progress, and so we just let her do that.

As I sit here with tears running down my cheeks, remembering these moments of being called to action, I recall how many there were. I had spent so much time swimming in the sea of ignorance as I began to learn how to be the best mother I could be to my special little girl. As she was born into a body that would fail her, so too had I been borne into a relationship where I was learning all over again how to be the best mum I could be, to a child with special needs. So much education was needed, not only for me, but Scott, and her nan who was her carer, when Scott and I were working. Same too for her sisters. The necessity to grow with the experience was crucial, to speak to doctors, to understand terminology, and diagnoses. To try new ways of feeding, and to connect to our senses so much more. The silent whimper from her bedroom in the dead of night could be a crucial moment in how her experience with us would play out. To wake to the smallest sounds and to notice the smallest changes in her persona, or her temperament. As you learn to embrace this very sensory way of nurture, you do grow, but you also make a lot of mistakes along the way.

Mother's guilt is a very real, and rapid emotion if you allow it to consume you. As a parent, not only to Bella, but my two eldest girls, I have made lots of mistakes. I have had to forgive myself for moments where perhaps I should have known more, done more, understood more. Falling down the stairs with Bella will stay with me forever. For a long time, the love in my heart was rattled by the thought that perhaps that was something I could have prevented.

There were more moments like that one, in my experience with Bella. The first time she had a seizure in my care will also remain embedded in my memories until the day I die. We had had our usual bath together that day. Bella loved having a bath with me. I feel that she enjoyed the sensation of floating in the water. Usually this would mean that I would lay down and she would lay between my legs, facing upwards, so that my hips could support her upper back and the lower part of her body could float, my hands holding hers. I would sing songs to her, and then sometimes she would lay on my chest, as encouragement for her to lift her head and strengthen her upper back with this action. We loved these moments together for the most part, with the water not too hot, but not too cold.

I had taken her out of the bath this day, and as I was carrying her to the lounge room where her clothes were laid out for her to be dressed in, she began to make peculiar sounds like a grinding in the back of her throat. Her body was becoming stiff. Fear ran through my veins, in that moment, like rampant fire. I placed her down on her side, thinking only of the tongue in her throat and how I did not want it to choke her. She zoned out, her eyes vacant for what seemed an eternity, but in its entirety only a couple of minutes. I was held to full attention in that moment. Full attention. 'Bella!' 'Bella!' 'Bella!' is all I could muster with fear piercing the air that we were held in. Her lips turning blue and her breathing vapid. She was still for what felt like an eternity, and then she returned to me with a gentle smile on her face, almost as if to say, 'okay, I'm ready to be dressed now Mum.'

Her eyes looking into mine, and that warm sound coming from her mouth brought me to tears, as the fear released from the valves of my heart. My heart ached as Bella lay comfortably on the lounge while I dressed her. My inner dialogue was filled with 'was the water warm enough?' 'was the water cool enough?' I moved between, 'had I kept her in too long?' and 'did I feed her something that might have triggered this onset?' The rambling went on and on as she shook her rattle and indulged in the elongated ears which she loved to chew, none the wiser to the emotions which were moving through my body.

Mother's guilt and hyper-vigilance are the perfect recipe for panic attacks and increased anxiety, I can tell you that much. Being constantly alert around not only the decisions you make just in the general care of your beautiful baby with special needs, but constantly waiting for the next moment where she may stop breathing, or may have a seizure, or was maybe not receiving enough of the CPAP support when she slept. Bella's journey moved me like tidal waves between petering on the edge of a nervous breakdown, and back to the depth of love, joy and inspiration in how amazing her heart and spirit expanded in the physical life with us.

I had to learn to manage tidal waves of emotion so that I could enjoy the life we had together whilst she was still with us. This was a difficult journey to meander through, with exceedingly difficult lessons to learn along the way, but I cannot even compare the difficult moments, to the abundance of love she brought to us, and received from us. The day she arrived in our lives changed us, just as the day she left shaped us differently. What a strong and magical teacher she was to us, as she taught us about humility, joy and love. The deepest ocean of love that you could ever imagine.

Suicide Dreaming

Naked
In the bath
Cold water
Cold like the heaviness of thunder
Rustling up the broken pieces of my heart.
Losing pieces
Finding pieces
Then losing them again
Suiciding the only escape
To the coldness of this water
Biting my skin

Phone a friend.

Let Me Out

IT'S INTERESTING WHEN days turn into nights and nights turn into days, and then it all just becomes one. Keeping busy and trying to get back into some form of routine when nothing is the same, and everything is changed, and there is no sense, only sorrow. You are numb at the same time and putting on smiles for people who do not really even matter. For those first two months after Bella died it felt like so many things were happening, but nothing was happening, all at the same time. Numbness and pain, progress but not really progress. I suppose my words reflect how little grounding there is in that initial space that follows losing a child.

So, when we had eventually begun to settle into our new home, the energy of pain began to push through the outer core of holding it together. The pain was so much stronger than any level of pretence that I could summon in any moment. Everything I looked at was dark with pain. Every breath hurt. Everything tasted like an end.

It was the day before Mahala's eighth birthday, 24th August 2016, that I woke up from a dream of pain, into a reality of pain. My children were with their fathers, and I was alone once again, in my house with stairs. Same style stairs as those that featured in another pain story in my thoughts. I ran a shallow bath because I was not bothered with a full one. I sat in it. I do not know how much time passed but there was no getting away from the ranting of a combined break in heart and mind telling me to die. Die. Die. Die. Nothing was worth living for. Suicide was the only way out of this pain that I was held in, held under, held down by. Dark and blackness everywhere in my thoughts; that looping cycle of thought that just would not leave me. I rattled through the options which were available to me. I could hang myself, but who would find me? What if one of my children found me, then I would damage them with that mental image forever. I could take pills, but do I have enough? These were the thoughts I could not escape from. The water was cold. I must have been engrossed in this fantasy of death for so long, yet still could not make the decision on how my life was going to end. Breathing was just a technicality by this stage, as my life was already over, I believed. The beautiful faces of my living daughters would filter intermittently through the darkness inside me, but I could not even cry for the shame that I felt seated in that cold water. I reached for my phone and sent a text to my beloved cousin by marriage Beck. 'I want to kill myself' is all it said.

The phone rang straight away, and on the other side were the words of one of the strongest women I know.

'You don't want to die my Tunny,' she said, and with that the floodgates opened. I could not stop the tears. She told me she was on her way and that I needed to get out of the bath. I do not remember getting out of the bath, or even getting dressed but I remember being on the couch when she arrived. I was unable to talk through the tears that were pouring down my face, and the sobs that had been held in for more than two months because I just was not able to completely release them. I asked Beck to take me to the hospital because I was afraid of what I would do. She lifted me from the couch with one arm, as she held her little baby in the other. Her son helped me to the vehicle. They buckled my seat belt as I attempted to catch breath between my sobs. I remember only a curtain of continuous tears over my eyes for the drive and then we were at the hospital in emergency. They put me in a room at the back of the emergency room. Beck went and saw the nurse, and my friend Lisa arrived.

A nurse came and sat with me and talked. I recall telling her that I was going to kill myself and that was when I contacted Beck. I then admitted myself to the Mental Health Ward at Wollongong Hospital. The doors shut behind me, and I stepped forward into the maze of my newest temporary residence.

The Forgotten

Screams of mayhem
Pierce these white walls
Where the empty echo of my shaken breaths
Become lost and alone,
Amidst
The clinical silencing
Of
The Forgotten

White Walls

HAVE YOU EVER spent time in a psych ward?

I am grateful that I landed between those white clinical walls of Wollongong's Mental Health Ward. Initially, as I entered the cold corridors of this forgotten place, a tiny whisper inside me reminded me that I didn't belong there, but the rattling and painful numbness of my body engulfed that whisper. Two nurses took me into the white small room which I would inhabit on my own and showed me the cupboard for my things before checking my clothes for anything that could be used as an instrument of suicide. They handed me a little cup with a sedative inside and a glass of water. They said goodbye as they left me there to absorb the painful whiteness of the room. The bed was hard, and the sheets were white and lifeless. I stood. I sat. I listened to the sounds of this place, as they slowly became louder and louder, from along the corridors and from the rooms which lined the corridor beside me.

Screams came from one end. A massive thud came from another, which I only imagined was someone running into a wall and falling to the floor. I felt petrified, and suddenly the warmth of my house, where I could not find any solace only hours before, seemed so much more inviting than this cold house of pain where I found myself, after asking to be brought here.

I lay down and I must have fallen asleep, although time was not something I was grasping as the sedative obviously did its job. I woke up, maybe a few hours later, and sat on my bed attempting to meditate, to draw my mind away from the anxious fear which began to engulf me, as I considered my options in this moment. Meditation was interrupted by more screams, and thuds and drugged inhabitants emptily walking the length of the corridor, up and down, up and down with no destination, not even inward it seemed.

I decided to go for a wander to explore this place. I left my room and walked out into the open area near the reception desk which was framed by glass screens with nurses seated behind them, waiting for the next enquiry to come forward from a heavily medicated resident. On the wall opposite the reception desk was a large poster of the earth which seemed to offer me an escape in my thoughts for a moment, to everywhere else I could be. A young lady with glazed over eyes joined me at this visual escape, with her eyes bearing into my soul. 'Hello' she said. The absence in her gaze triggered compassion in me for a moment as I thought about how young she appeared, and I considered how she had come to be here. She told me she was 21 and that she was schizophrenic. She got straight into her diagnosis, inviting me to give her mine so we could be bonded by our mental health issues. As I contemplated how I would present my situation in a one-word answer to the curiosity that shouted from her face, she told me that she had been in the mental health ward for months. MONTHS! How could this be, I thought to myself. I began to question quietly in my mind, what had happened in her life for her to be here at 21, and was the medication being administered helping her cause or her mental state and how was that outcome in front of me informing me of how my experience was going to go?

Survival mode kicked in rapidly for me as I continued to meander through conversation with this young resident of the mental health ward. Adrenalin fuelled my want to escape, with words strong in my mind that I did not belong in the mental ward of Wollongong hospital! I belonged with my family. My grieving children. I belonged with them. I needed to be with them. I belonged with my beautiful 7-year-old daughter whose birthday was the next day. Sarcastically, I pondered what a great story that would be that on her 8th birthday, her mother confined to a mental hospital because she could not find peace in the pieces of her broken heart, as grief was all encompassing! Survival mode. Adrenalin. It's amazing what the mind can pull off, even when the heart is shattered.

I took myself over to the nurses' station and told one of the nurses that I did not belong in the mental health ward, and that I was ready to sign myself out. I thought because I had admitted myself to hospital that this would be as easy as signing on the dotted line, calling Beck to come and collect me, and saying goodbye to the cold white walls of this establishment. But by the look on the nurse's face as I spoke to her, I knew straight away what was about to come out of her mouth.

'Unfortunately, that's not how this works Michelle,' she said as she looked me dead in the eyes, not even blinking. She continued to explain how, even though I had admitted myself to the ward, I would need clearance from a doctor before I could leave, and that if I continue to persist with asking the nurses to leave, I would only be kept here longer. My will to escape became almost panic, as I looked at all the other medicated souls walking aimlessly around the space. I questioned in my mind if this was how they started here, and all the sedatives had resulted in them being here for months, maybe years on end! I retreated to my room and cried. I needed to get back to my family.

The hours blended into one another. I asked if I could make a call. I approached the lonely black phone in the corner and rang Mahala to tell her that I may not be able to see her for her birthday the next day because I was at the hospital, but I was trying to get there and that I would call her the next day to wish her happy birthday. I hung up the phone and noticed the line to the cafeteria beginning to fill as food was being served. I meandered over and joined the queue, heavy in my step, but hungry too. For a moment I was reminded of the boarding school cafeteria; selecting the tray and perusing the food on offer as you giggle and laugh with your mates while contemplating the fun on the weekend. This was kind of the same, except vastly different in its context and not much laughter taking place. I gathered the food that was on offer and sat at a table with a man whose name I forget. We ate in silence.

A nurse approached me. A different nurse to the one who blankly painted a picture of my demise a while before. She sat with me and mentioned that the nurse I had spoken to earlier had told her of my request to leave. She engaged in conversation with me, asking me questions about myself and how I had come to be there. It felt like she may have been feeling me out, to determine whether I was actually plagued by mental illness and to figure out the next way forward. She was a godsend, and I told her how my heart was shattered in a million pieces, and that although I had had suicidal thoughts, I knew that I needed help. I asked her how I would be able to get home to my family. She was kind and told me that the doctor would be attending the ward the next day, and that I should have someone come along to vouch for me, and my sanity. My parents had moved from Melbourne to the Illawarra by this stage, and I knew if I called them, they would attend the appointment with me and the doctor the next day. I could possibly be free of this place, to begin my life over again, now that I had had a very real glimpse into what caged looked and felt like, I knew my Bella would not want me caged within these walls, where the immaculate gifts of the senses, in their free-flowing expression could not be experienced, lived and appreciated. All I had to do was get through the night in this space of emptiness. Tomorrow would be a day I could start again. To begin to heal my own chaotic emptiness which lurked all around and within me.

Beck had returned to visit me that night. We sat in the lounge room area with about ten or so residents of the ward. Between random swearing and cursing, and one older lady rubbing her vagina on the arm of the chair and gagging to vomit, we were able to have some conversation and give thanks for the life we had outside of this place. I felt sadness in my heart for the human beings that I was sharing this space with. They seemed to be forgotten.

Before bed I decided to do some yoga out in an open area that was adjacent to the loungeroom area Beck and I had sat in earlier. I was joined by a lovely lady with dark hair, who did not speak much, but put all her effort into downward dogs and upward dogs. She giggled like a little girl every now and then as she swore in whispers in a happy tone.

I thanked her for joining me and made my way to my room, where lights out was eventually signalled. My head hit the pillow with a prayer to the universe to stay with me as I moved into tomorrow. Blue torch lights intermittently woke me through the night as they were shone through the glass pane of the locked door to my room. Checking I was still alive perhaps. I am not sure.

The next day my parents arrived to give testimony to my sanity, and that of my safety. The Indian doctor, my parents, a nurse and myself all entered a small room with comfortable armchairs where we discussed the possibility of my leaving the mental health ward. Of course, my parents vouched for me, but I still had this fear that somehow something would inhibit my leaving this place. Perhaps I was afraid that they would see that deep inside me, I was empty. Broken. That the path ahead of me was a long one, and that I did not really know how I was going to survive the missing. I knew that I wanted to survive. That was the gift from the mental health ward.

The doctor confirmed that I was grieving, I was not insane. My parents reassured the doctor that they had my best interests at heart, and the nurse, well she did not say much.

I was free to leave.

That night, I returned to my home, and ran myself a bath. A fuller bath than the one that had held me captive the day before. I made it hot, and I stepped into it with the visualisation of washing away the experience of death that had been looming in my thoughts. I soaked there for some time. After I emerged, I dressed in warm comfy clothes, descended the stairs and lit some incense to try to initiate calm in my experience. I relished the small pleasures that I had not been able to feel the peace and beauty in only 48 hours before.

I sat down on my couch and wrote a list titled 'Pro's Non-Suicide List'! It seemed fitting to write down all the benefits of not having killed myself the day before. It was difficult to write, because I had to remember, in the gloomy hollow of my mind, the gifts of my life and myself. I managed to write down 11 pros to being alive.

1. 2 amazing kids who love me so much.
2. Cool new place to share with family, and friends and cat.
3. I can finally surf a wave. Taken me ages. Conquering fears one at a time.
4. I am talented in lots of areas: writing, yoga, business minded.
5. I get to spend more time with my friends. They rock.
6. There is always help. Just ask.
7. Plenty of fish in the sea.
8. So many more sunny days.
9. So many more cozy days.
10. So many adventures to be had.
11. Not even 40 yet!!

I kept the list. It's a wonderful reminder of choice, and time and all that comes about based on those two very crucial factors. It brought me back to the present moment that was both vapid and excruciating and therefore overtly confusing as my heart was shattered, but it also allowed me to feel that eventually I would experience hope again.

Panic in the Dark

Three dark strangers
Arrived in shadow form.
They lingered in the dark of night,
Of my panic they were borne.
No words were ever spoken,
Only a gesture to my heart.
That a break was coming for this place
That would tear my world apart.

Held in the Hand of Spirit

I AM A positive person most of the time. I can say authentically now, that my positivity is held in truth and light, and my darkness held in the same. I have spent a large part of my life masking my pain with busyness and counterfeit smiles, because like so many, there are lots of pain stories in my life with the loss of my Bella the greatest.

I was raised in a Catholic home in Zululand, a district of KwaZulu Natal, in South Africa. We attended church most Sundays. The final school I went to for year 11 and 12 was a Convent, with fully fledged nuns and a priest who was difficult to understand. This consistent push from a spiritual sector that I did not resonate with, created a retaliation in me that urged me to discover my own faith. To connect to, and be guided by my own intuition as I stumbled at times through understanding that which could not be seen. What a profound and powerful concept faith is! An energy which breeds so much contention, and war and suffering in the world whilst still holding hearts in a place of safety and security in their lives.

Bella's natural way of being in this world with the love that reached from her heart and her eyes, and the gentle yet fierce tenacity of her soul, brought a love purer than we, as her greatest supporters, had ever experienced in our lives. I speak only here for myself and my two older children. A love that was not expressed by words, as she could not speak them; or bold physical expressions, as she could not muster them. It was a love that she felt, and gave to us through her pores, her eyes, her expression, her heart and mind combined. She taught us this love, and how to return it. She taught us how to pass it on to others. She taught us how to hold people that we love safely in this space. Such a little body with such a massive and powerful soul. A spiritual experience far beyond any other that I have ever experienced in my lifetime, and probably ever will again. A love that taught me lessons I will carry so deeply inside me through this life, and possibly into the next if I am afforded one.

She existed from her heart, as that was her means of communication. By doing so she presented herself to this world in a physical body which would eventually fail her, but a spiritual connection to life and existence that opened our hearts up to the same.

When a soul loves you this way, you open more too. You begin to open more to the possibilities that exist beyond the physical. Your heart opens to love, the connection to nature more than ever, and to the realms outside of what is seen. Bella was a major catalyst for this opening in me, as through this deeply sensory love, my own intuition and understanding became a major guide for me. Bella's experience with us opened this channel of knowing even more. It's a love which is sensory, profoundly intuitive in its nurture and deepens the experience of existing in this realm of life.

I awoke in the dark of night to see three tall and dark shadows standing beside my bed in the darkness of the hour when spirits are most 'alive', I knew the message they were bringing me was one of pain. It was May 2016. Bella had depleted so much up until that point, her manner was lethargic and the weight of her body falling from her bones. The protrusion of her bones against her skin was frightening at times as I watched her ribs expand as she breathed. There was little flesh beneath her skin to comfort them.

On this night in May, I had decided to let Bella sleep with me. To keep her extra close. Her hand held in mine as we sometimes slept. I had been filled with worry. There was a persistent nudging and knowing that would not leave my body. My baby was vanishing before my eyes. I fell asleep to the sound of those worrying words in my mind and awoke hours later with only the limited expression of light from the bathroom seeping through my door, framing the tall dark shadows that stood beside my bed. My eyes were wide open as I followed the length of their form, with no faces I could see, only an extended arm of blackness reaching to my chest and placing pressure to the point that I was struggling to breathe. Bella's name attempted to heave from my chest, leave my mouth and call out to her. I looked over to my left to see her sleeping peacefully beside me. As I returned my gaze to the shadows to my right, the weight on my chest released and the shadows were no longer there.

A deep sense of sorrow enveloped me, as I felt that something terrible was coming. The panic which had sent sirens through my mind prior to sleep, personified in form as I woke in the dark of that night.

I awoke the next morning and tried to forget the feeling I had felt through the night, and the message in the darkness I had received. A silent nudge from the universe to be prepared for something, not completely knowing what, but to honour the moments even more with this knowing.

We continued, and all that I have shared before progressed as it did.

So, when I stepped out of the psychiatric ward of Wollongong Hospital with an adrenalin-fuelled want to survive, greater than I had experienced in the previous two months, I felt a need to connect to that love Bella left us with. A love so pure. The place healing and living is most beautifully expressed. I knew I had to find that light again, but this time in myself.

Bella's birthday was approaching. On the 30th September 2011 our beautiful angel arrived in this world in her frail little body, not breathing but fighting to do the work she was sent here to do. I felt I needed to honour her on this day as she would have been five on 30th September 2016. A celebration of her spirit it would be, to be shared with all the beautiful women in my life, who held me so safely through this great period of loss.

Scott and I had decided that we would spread Bella's ashes on this day too at the water's edge of Sharkies beach in Coledale. We felt it was the perfect gift to release the physical cremains of her body to be free to swim with the Great Mother and explore the tides of this world.

I invited the special and beautiful women in my life, and along with Bella's sisters at my side, we would celebrate beautiful Bella with a Sisterhood Circle on sunrise. The beauty of her day would be welcomed, bound by the powerful feminine energy of this circle.

The morning of the 30th arrived. The invitation was for all who attended, to bring along some colourful flowers to gift to our Great Mother after our ceremony, placing them in her waters, thanking her for her presence, and for receiving my baby as she would that day. We approached the beach with very few words spoken, as the stillness of dawn was upon us, carrying our flowers and love in our hearts. Our circle took form, and as we welcomed each other to this place, we connected through breath and holding hands to allow our energy to bind us in this ceremony. To connect us strongly to source and breathe in our intentions for this day. To give my Bel the gift of our love and presence for her birthday.

The universe provided the most amazing sunrise that morning. Those who sat in the circle with their backs to the horizon turned to face the beauty of the display. We took in each shape, each shift in colour, each breath of the breeze. The dance of the sun's rays projected the most magnificent display before us, before the Great Sun began to appear above the line of the horizon.

Three beautiful women in our circle shared words, poems and expressions of their love. We cried. We laughed. We rejoiced at the beauty of the morning we were so apart of. The energy of the morning was holding us, and we were holding the energy of the morning too.

Following our Sisterhood Circle our gifts of flowers were released to the water's edge allowing the tides to gently pull them away from us. We returned to the shore to say our goodbyes. As friends left with joy in their hearts, my girlfriend Stacey showed me the images she had captured of our morning. There behind myself and my two girls, was a beautiful round green orb of energy, floating.

I would like to think that was Bella's spirit with us that morning. Dancing in the frosty breeze, free and abundant in her abilities. I have no doubt she was smiling. Joyful. Her spirit welcomed by the openness of our hearts in the first light of that day.

The final gift in our birthday celebration was releasing the last of Bella's physical presence to the ocean, to swim with the Great Mother. Scott came down to join us at Sharkies Beach carrying Bella's ashes. Our daughters and I joined him at the rocks edge. We released the ashes from the white PVC container that held them, and wished her well as the ashes and the flower's we gifted before, became one with the tides.

It was a beautiful birthday celebration for our girl.

Drowning

The salt
It seeped
It rolled
It fell
It pooled in my heart
Forming a well

I lingered
I stayed
It hurt
I sunk
My limbs were limp
No fight in their tread

Deeper the salt
Invited me in
I opened my eyes
To find where the end would begin
I tilted my head
To look down below
And there in the depth
The beginning
It glowed

I breathed in the salt
To strengthen my grasp
My toes, they pointed
To reach the light at last
The light filtered through
My limbs felt anew
My gaze lifted high
The light above shone through

The rhythm of my heart
Found a stronger beat
I pulled and pulled
My arms strong once again
The dark well released me
As I fought to the end

I breathed in the air
Fresh from above
I opened my mouth
To release the heaviness of love
I floated a while
To feel the sun on my face
The depth beneath me
Released me with grace

I smiled
I surrendered
To the battle and the win
Here is where the end
Became the new journey
To begin

One Step Forward, Two Steps Back

I FELT SO connected to my love for Bella during and after her birthday ceremony. So connected to her, her love, her light. But that is the clincher with grief. It is a torrid sea with many waves and tumultuous tides. Staying connected to the beautiful feelings of love is exceedingly difficult, and possibly not where the healing begins, I soon came to understand. The opportunity for deep and cellular healing exists in feeling into the dark side of having loved so deeply and so maternally. Travelling with awareness into the deep well of chaos and mayhem which is left from such an experience, to find the light again.

I did not completely understand this at the beginning. I was impulsive at times in my want for the pain to stop. I wanted to feel the euphoria of that love holding me through the days so I could just heal already. How selfish I was in those thoughts at times. But also, how ignorant and unaware I was too. How conditioned I was to believe that I was meant to just get up and get on with my life, because that was what I had always done. I hadn't been completely educated on how to deal with the tragedies of life, and the ripple effects from an emotional, spiritual and physical perspective, and bring them into a long-term pattern of living. But then again, how do you ever consciously prepare for the loss of your child? There is no preparation for such a tragedy.

My soul knew that there was lots more work to be done, but the mother in me also recognised that I had to be okay for my two beautiful daughters who were still here with me. They needed me to be strong. They had held me so safely for the first six months after Bella's passing. It was not until I started to see the cracks of their grief and love emerging, that I realised waves of pain were continuously vibrating through our little unit, and that there was so much work to do.

Mahala, Kai and I began to see a therapist. An intelligent, colourful and vibrant lady who engaged so well with them both, especially through pictures, colours and expression. She opened conversations and we managed to talk more about our grief and our missing. Starting this process of doing the actual clinical work around our loss was a really important step, and one I continue to do today.

For the first six months after Bella passed, Mahala and Kai did all they could from their hearts to make sure that I was okay. The tender nurture of their love reached as far into my space as it could, to check in with me and to give me love. As I reflect, I felt I had no strength in me to even muster being the mum I was before Bella passed. How could I be when the person I was before died with her on that painful day, and only darkness remained. But, after that six-month period, I began to witness my girls' grief coming to the surface. What a call to action that was, even though I had little strength of my own.

Mahala's pain began to manifest in the form of alopecia. At first only a small patch of baldness appeared at the top of her head, in amongst her beautiful and thick mane of hair. After that first patch of baldness appeared, it wasn't long before the alopecia began to spread, and she soon had very large patches of baldness all over her beautiful 8-year-old head. It was a quiet blessing that she still had enough hair to cover most of those patches. Mahala is a private soul, and having people ask questions about what was happening would have been an experience even more conflicting and uncomfortable for her. I would like to add here, Mahala has consented to me sharing this part of her journey, once again her strength and maturity shining through.

One morning, after months of treatment with a dermatologist which resulted in scabs that had formed on Mahala's bald patches, I was trying to do her hair for school as gently as possible so as not to hurt her or aggravate the painful scabs, she said to me, 'Mum, can you home school me?' 'Of course,' I answered. I tried to comfort her by letting her know that although I did not believe all her hair was going to fall out, that if it happened to, we would shave my head too, and we could be baldies together. She seemed to like that I was trying to put a bit of humour into the moment, but deep inside I knew that this situation was very confusing for her.

It was about this time in our journey, Mahala expressed her desire to do horse riding lessons. Another call to action!! So that is exactly what we did! I was petrified of horses but had heard so much about equine therapy and the beautiful nurture of these animals. The horse-riding journey began. Mahala loved her sessions, and eventually signed up for Saddle Club, which was a four-year program. She still loves riding horses to this day, and even managed to convince me to get on and have a go. We now own and love our own horse, Brandy. She has been a wonderful part of both Mahala and my healing journey.

It took about 9 months for the alopecia to heal, with intermittent bald spots coming through only sporadically over the next year, but it eventually healed. I cannot explain my joy when one morning whilst carrying out my usual inconspicuous 'new hair' checks whilst doing Mahala's hair for school, I noticed growth! This had been such a long and painful experience for Mahala and finally the energetic effort, patience and strength which she had invested at such a young age was paying off. The medicine and her own personal healing modality, horse riding, had begun to impact her nervous system, energy and heart positively, and we were shown some light. I started crying as I expressed how happy I was that there was growth. She tried to stay contained, but there was joy in that beautiful heart shining through her eyes.

Kai's cracks began to show in her 15th year of life. Kai's natural temperament is one of joy, love and happiness. She was, and still is the soul that will give her love so easily. She lights up a room with her joy and is the most beautiful friend and sister you could imagine. But when she was 15 her mental anguish was so entangled in the feelings of loss of her sister, they became too much for her to bare. I tried to understand the changes in her that I could see, and the sadness in her that I could feel, and she tried to hide what she was feeling but her natural way disappeared before me in that year. Depression became her dark cloud. She tried to numb the pain that she was experiencing by self-harming. It was not until I discovered an open diary with her blood on it and found some very painful words from her heart written on those pages, that I understood how much of that pain she was carrying and not sharing with me. Initially all my questions and concerns only made her retreat further into herself, as she tried to process what was happening for her. It was an exceedingly difficult journey, but eventually she found the strength to ask for help. She began to share her feelings around what she was experiencing. To cry, deep, long cries.

I am so proud of my girls for the courage they connected to in themselves, when all darkness was coming over them. Each of these beautiful young women navigated through vastly different manifestations of their grief, however both came back to the love in their hearts eventually. What beautiful teachers our children are.

I have learnt so much through this journey and understand that though the wound may not be your fault, healing is certainly your responsibility. In my own journey from there to here, I have tried my best to reflect this responsibility to them. I lead by example in as many ways as I can, but still reflect authenticity in that, at times there are entrapments to being a human being. We stumble and fall and start all over again.

In the following months, and even years, after Bella's death I tried to ride the waves of unconditional love that still resided in the energy she left, but still there was a wound so deep inside me that I was unable to access.

I noticed how escapism was a definite go-to for me in a bid to keep me safe from really going deep into that place where the puss of pain was residing, slowly poisoning more and more the way my mind worked, or the way in which I presented myself to the world.

Escapism is a very real concept. Whether its sex, drugs, alcohol or exercise, sometimes fear encourages an impulsive way out of a very necessary situation. With any deep core wound, there is only so much you can play on the surface before the toxicity of the wound is revealed and you must go back to the drawing board. Repeating the same behaviours always brings about the same result. I am guilty of this loop in behaviour, and it always brings me back to the same place. To the wound! The deep well of darkness is where the healing should have begun. Upon reflection I needed to take the long way around. To repeat the same mistakes and to trip myself up time and time again so I could completely understand the path I was on, and the journey that lay before me.

Escapism also became a way of me avoiding what I knew would make me feel the emotion of my emptiness. I found methods to express myself through writing and used social media as a layer of protection, to be just another human amongst hundreds of other humans expressing themselves. Of course, people do engage on this platform, but it is so instantaneous that to be seen is fleeting and it allowed me to express and release. The positive part of this path in escapism is that I began to connect to my pain through words, to slowly dive deeper into that darkness, to feel my emotions as they moved through my body to my fingertips and onto a screen or a piece of paper.

So many nights I would cry myself to sleep and wake the next morning to a life that I did not completely understand, but had to for the sake of my children, and for the sake of the career I had, and for the bills I was paying. I waited for next night out, when my children were not with me, and for the hangover I would experience so I could just feel like death because death is what lingered in my thoughts and in my heart.

Grief is a never ending well if you are prepared to go into it. It invites you to either dive right the hell in and feel so much pain and suffering until you reach a place of light, or it scares you into just skimming the surface, back pedalling on the surface of suffering and living a mediocre life with no connection to a greater source at all; just toxic situations with toxic outcomes.

Grief presents you with massive choices as to how your life will move forward, just as love does. It's in the awareness of your grief that you begin to slowly emerge from the shadows of pain in that experience.

Sugarman

Consciousness and Anxiety
Sat down one day for tea.
One was warm and blissful,
The other jittery.
Consciousness delighted in the peace of the Spring time air
Anxiety came charging with lengthy verbal despair,
Over all that was lacking
In the air of that space.
How the silence was deafening
How the tea was too strong
How she was not worthy
How she did not belong.

Consciousness just breathed,
Drawing in, releasing out.
She listened with heart, intently
To Anxiety's tortured shout.
She leaned in with love from her eyes,
And in her humble tone
Offering peace and safety
As Anxiety's new home.

Anxiety began to cry,
Defeated in herself.
Through heavy tears she lifted,
Her gaze to Consciousness.
Her jaw too locked to tremble
Tension, a tightening leash
Consciousness sang softly
To soften Anxiety's speech.

Consciousness and Anxiety
Sat down to tea this day.
Anxiety, seeking refuge
From the mental games at play.
Consciousness hummed Rodrigues,
As her melodic sip and sway.
Anxiety surrendered,
With Consciousness leading the way.

Preparation

FOR A FEW years prior to 2016, I made sure I gave myself a spiritual retreat every year. Something that honoured the connection I had to my soul, the energy in my body, and the learning which I yearned for in this area. I had been a yoga teacher and meditation teacher for many years and working with my body opened me up to more awareness practices, strength in my body and mind and to the healing benefits of meditation. I would make provisions for this learning and honour myself with time just for me. I loved the connection to spirit, and the journey of discovering this path deeper and deeper inside myself.

2015 had been a challenging, beautiful and overwhelming year. I was working part time for the government and had set up a cleaning business to try and supplement my income, as the rent in our beautiful flat house in Woonona was higher than what we were previously paying. The benefits of living in that beautiful flat house, far outweighed the stress of having to make extra money. I was teaching yoga to supplement my income even more, so I could not only give myself the spiritual retreat I needed that year, but also provide my children with a fun and relaxing holiday too. I took all three of my girls on an adventure to Queensland for the first time all together. Bella and Mahala's nan had come with us, and we had a beautiful holiday. I loved our road trips together. They were filled with laughter and singing for the most part, with Kai being the perfect navigator to my left as I drove.

It was the year we had been assigned a Case Manager from Mission Australia to assist us in managing the requirements of Bella's ongoing needs and care, and the year that Bella's orthopaedic surgeon began to engage in conversations with us, around options to help rectify her spine, which was becoming more and more impacted by the strain of kyphosis and scoliosis. Initially Dr Grey had suggested leg splints to help with the positioning of Bella's legs too, however with so much to consider relating to her spine, he suggested we hold off on her leg splints for a short time. There was so much to consider in these moments, and so many new experiences that were required with Bella's care. We trialled a hoist that year too at our flat house in Woonona. I remember being so grateful that this wonderful piece of equipment was going to be provided to us. To help us care for our littlest love and to provide safe and secure lifting of her growing body. It also impacted my mind, as it was another particularly important step on a journey that did not provide any answers past the exact moment that we were in. All I could do was be grateful and try and not let the complexities of all the questions that wanted to impact my experience, come through.

Like I said it was a big year, so I decided to book in for a Vipassana Buddhist 10-day silent retreat in Tasmania at the end of that full year. This retreat drew me in, not only for the challenge of complete silence for 10 days in monk-style accommodation in the Tasmanian forest, but also that it was a donation-based retreat. To pay what you could. This resonated with me immensely as I was a single mother with an income which was not dispensable.

I left for the retreat on Boxing Day, with my duffle camo bag over my shoulder. I caught a train to the airport and got on that plane with great excitement at the prospect of thirteen days for me. Sometimes I think, as parents, we are guilted into believing that we cannot make time for ourselves to replenish and heal. With mothers' guilt hot on my tail, there was still a sense of relief of being alone, knowing I was giving myself time, and spiritual connection, to replenish and learn about myself. I arrived in beautiful Tassie, and made my way to my booked accommodation in Hobart. I had purposefully arrived the day before my retreat began, and gave myself an extra day on the other side of the retreat experience, to explore a bit more of this gorgeous holding of Mother Nature.

My accommodation was a gorgeous little unit with the harbour not far down the end of the road. I decided to go exploring after I checked in. I walked down towards the water's edge with a little hip-hop in my step, feeling the breeze of a new place on my face, and exploration at my feet. I heard music coming from down the way, just near the water and found a pub with a bustle of energy and life, and the smell of steak oozing from the windows. I was hungry. I made friends very quickly and came to realise that Tasmania is a very friendly place. I danced and drank and moved into midnight with not a care in the world for that moment, but when my alarm went off at 7 am that next morning reminding me I had a bus to catch to a meditation retreat, I did hold some regret.

Everyone else seemed so vibrant and engaged on the small 13-seater bus, whereas I was hungover and probably had a nice scent of Jack Daniels seeping from my pores. As the twelve of us left Hobart on the little bus, I let my head fall to the window and closed my eyes, hoping the bed would be comfortable where we were heading.

When I opened my eyes again, we were entering a winding road, with tall, beautiful trees aligning the bitumen. We headed deeper and deeper into the forest, and although my hangover was still looming, I felt a lifting sense of excitement as the calling of the earth resonated with my purpose of being in that very location at that exact moment. Soon after, the bus arrived at the Dhamma Pabha Vipassana Meditation Centre, Tasmania. A very modest holding nestled in a forest in the slopes of Mount Dromedary, with only the sounds of native wildlife surrounding it.

I stepped from the bus, grabbed my duffle bag and entered the humble space where we were directed to the common area for a debriefing and guidance on how the residential retreat would run. The rules of the residency for the ten-day period were that male and female accommodation were separate. No eye contact was to be made. No talking, no reading, no writing, no phones and no masturbation. I'll be honest and say that when that last rule was expressed, I wondered to myself, 'would they know?' The program commenced with meditation at 4am and ended at 9pm in the evening with three breaks during the day. A total of eleven hours of meditation a day. We were shown to our rooms, which were basic monk-style accommodation. A bed, a side table, and a cup to catch spiders. The cup created some anxiety in my body, but luckily, I did not have to catch any spiders for the time I was there.

The process of meditation began that evening, with the practice of Vipassana given only in the third day. Vipassana is a specific meditation practice where you hold a one-pointed space of awareness without being deterred by bodily sensations. This practice requires the practitioner to sit in a comfortable seated position and move the awareness of the mind from the crown of the head all the way down to the toes in inch size increments along the entire length of the body, and then all the way back up again to the crown of the head. The practice continues in this way over and over and over, all day. If a distraction of sensation or something else takes the mind from the practice, the practitioner needs to start again from the very top of the head, and move all the way down the body in the same way.

As you can imagine, at first the practice of Vipassana would be intriguing to someone who is interested in developing deeper sense of awareness on the spiritual path. By day two my excitement at being in this beautiful humble space was still present, although I was feeling the aches and pains of sitting for these long periods of time. But I was not going to break! You see, if you leave the retreat during the practice, you can't come back, and I didn't want to be that guy!

The days continued. On day three we began the practice of Vipassana and with intrigue and focus day three moved into day four. The centre offered bolsters, blankets and other props to provide some comfort to maintain the practice. Some visitors to the space chose to kneel in the meditative state, others chose to sit with support behind their backs and under their knees. The meditation hall was about 100 metres away from the accommodation and was simple in its construction and form, matching that of the sleeping quarters. The routine was much the same every day with a 4 am start of meditation, breakfast, meditation, lunch, meditation, dinner, meditation and bedtime.

It was on day five that I noticed a shift in my level of awareness. Yes, I was maintaining the practice of Vipassana, however something else was taking place within my psychic body and my energetic body. I began to feel and see in my mind's eye, the rise and fall of specific and deep trauma stories coming to the surface for me to look at, acknowledge and let go. It was like these trauma stories laid themselves on the shore of perception, one at a time, and then retreated into the deep space of consciousness. At first when I noticed this, it distracted my mind from the practice of Vipassana and I swore to myself as I had to start again from the crown of my head. But, this also brought a sense of joy to have worked into this next state of the experience. I began again at the crown of my head and continued with the practice. Different stories of my life arose and fell, and as I kept the practice of

Vipassana consistent, I noticed that without attaching to these painful past stories, I was able to witness them falling back and disappearing.

I went to bed that night after eleven hours of seated meditation, my body feeling tired, but energised. I couldn't wait to experience the lessons which day six would bring forward. The hand-held bell rang in the early hours of the following day, and we all walked up in silence to the meditation hall and assumed the positions we were holding for our pre-breakfast meditation. The practice began, and I was able to connect more deeply and sooner to this meditative state than I had the day before. As I retreated deeper and deeper into the state of meditation, and as the stories of my beautiful Bella's pain and struggles began to lift from the depth of my soul, the tears just flowed from my eyes. I stayed in the practice as a witness to all that was arising from our experience, with the abundance of pain, stories from her birth to the new struggles that she had faced that year, were reflected continuously all of day six. I cried so much that day in that seated space, but as I was held in this beautiful practice, I released so much of that pain. I released the pain of watching her struggle. Of her seizures which bred the fear of loss into my heart. Watching her suffer, but still laugh and smile, even with a sore tummy where the acid reflux was burning her little belly. Day six was my day of witness and release as my soul prepared for the journey to come.

I believe I was meant to be there at that time, to understand more deeply how energy moves through this capsule that our souls encompass, and to experience this ceremony of preparation presented by the Universe. To understand more about how we hold pain, and how deeply that pain can be pushed down and ignored through the everyday experiences of life. I was guided to that place, so I would be able to live through her loss. I believe this completely.

There were many more experiences of opening and understanding which came from attending Vipassana in the Mount Dromedary Forest in Tasmania, but day six was my Bella day. It was the day I was able to witness all that I had suppressed through 'getting things done' and pushing the pain down through existing. I was able to experience a clearing of pain, so I could work through the pain of what was coming.

I must reflect on just how beautiful this experience was for me as a human being, as a mother, and as a spiritual creature always looking to understand and grow, even when I make silly choices. Being held in this beautiful practice for those 10 days, within a magical forest, was one of the greatest gifts I have ever given to myself. I returned to my children refreshed, focused and ready to tackle all that was coming, just in the everyday challenges which Bella's condition presented. When I returned, my children saw that I was ready and able to seize the days, and explore and adventure with them. That too felt like a gift from the universe. I understand more so now, how important it is as an individual to have alone time, to discover pathways to better understanding of this life, and how the ripple effect of self-love and nurture impacts those we love in a positive way too.

The Shape of You

There's a YOU shape,
The shape of you.
It's the hole that was left,
As you passed through.

I have stared at it.
Coloured it.
Painted it blue.
But it's still a YOU shape,
The shape of YOU.

I have loved it,
And honoured it.
Tried to fix it,
It's true.
But, the hole
Is still a YOU shape,
The shape of YOU.

Another year has passed,
Passed on through.
Never forgotten
Is the beauty and love of YOU.
The light keeps shining,
As we continue.
With this YOU shaped hole inside us.
Missing YOU.

Rituals and Revelations

EVER SINCE OUR Sisterhood Circle, my daughters and I have continued with our ritual of visiting the water's edge, where Bella's ashes were spread at Sharkies Beach. Our ritual encompasses her day of birth and her day of death. The day she arrived and the day she left. The first couple of years were a difficult celebration of her beautiful soul, but a celebration of our love nonetheless. Every year still to this day, we take her flowers and give them with love to the sea, to honour the Great Mother who holds her physical and her spiritual presence, and to gift her with the colour of those petals.

This ritual is our connection to love, and a space we will continue to honour until our last days. A pathway to connect to her in our hearts and make room for those feelings of grief, but more so of the love that we feel for our beautiful Bella.

Every year since she left, the day before her day of birth, and her day of death, are always the most difficult for me. But I allow them to be difficult. I allow myself to cry and feel and lean into that space in my womb where our cells became one, where our hearts beat as one and where my blood was her blood until she had her own. I allow and honour those tears to fall, as much as they need to.

The first-year anniversary of her death held me with deep intensity. My thoughts tempered around how twelve months could have passed so quickly, yet so slow in its effect. My womb pulsed and ached. Deep pains of sadness vibrated from the inside out, with my tears the final release as my jaw clenched and ached. The day before the anniversary of her death unravelled me the most. The looming doom which existed in all of me, the ever-present succumbing to what completely was. My loss, and our Great Mother's gain.

Bella's sisters had chosen to sleep with me that night on the first anniversary of her passing. We would do this often, seeking comfort in each other's warmth, and in knowing we were safe in each other's love. Also, in their view, Mum's bed is the comfiest. Even though my bedroom was a garage converted, and theirs the nicest rooms in the house, they preferred to be in with me that night.

My heavy heart nestled into deep sorrow for all that had passed before that night as I surrendered into the softness of my mattress, my lips and my tongue the final resting place for my tears.

I woke to the sound of tapping which brought me out of my deep sleep, and into a place of needing to adjust to the darkness in my room. I sat up to the sound, searching for an explanation to the persistent sound of tapping, like on glass only more to the right of my gaze, and calling for my attention. From my bed I turned to follow what I thought must be a dreamy discovery of Holly our cat up on the kitchen bench being sneaky. But as I looked, I was greeted by the face of a woman staring straight at me from outside, framed behind the glass of the kitchen window above the sink. Her face clear and her intention persistent.

My fear was fixated on her face. She was older, with brown shoulder length hair and a fringe. She continued to tap on the window with a stern singular finger, and noticing she had caught my attention, she motioned with her hand for me to come to her.

My heart began to beat with a fierceness that I had only ever felt once or twice before, pumping the energy of fear through my veins. The heat radiated from my body as I froze for a moment, considering what the next step from here would be. Our eyes were still fixed. She continued to motion me towards her as my legs, unwilling, stepped out one by one from the bed, preparing to walk towards this lady in the night whose face I had never seen before.

As I stood in the doorway of my garage-converted bedroom with her eyes still fixated on mine, her mouth began to create the shapes to hold the words of 'come here Michelle'. I was so held in fear I didn't even consider that somehow, this stranger knew my name. My eyes widened to capture a second figure standing beside her. This figure however was just the shape of a human with no facial features that I could see. His energy masculine, with broad shoulders, and a grey warm undertone to his aura. He spoke no words.

I was crying by this stage, but my legs continued to walk towards her. I took a step up from my bedroom to the entry of the kitchen, tears falling fast from my eyes, as I responded to her words that I was scared and that I did not want to. Her mouth returned the softening of 'don't be afraid, just come'.

I continued along past the kitchen bench, towards the sliding door which exited out to the courtyard of our townhouse. As I approached the door, I stopped a couple of metres away to find that my courtyard was jam packed full of figures resembling the older lady's companion. So many faceless, energetic bodies were facing in my direction, as the closest figure motioned with his hand for me to open the sliding door. Once again, the energy was masculine in its feel. My tears were still flowing, as I spoke out to the sea of faceless bodies that I was afraid. 'Don't be afraid Michelle,' The sound vibrated through the glass. With a softening into surrender, I stepped forward and opened the door.

The vacuum of energy was like something I have never felt before, as flashes moved at light speed past me. To the left and to the right of me, the faceless bodies one by one overflowed into my home as I stood motionless, held within their entry. I recognised that this experience was something far beyond what I had felt or seen before. An awakened state within dream time, yet such a poignant moment.

As the energetic souls entered in haste, the older lady from the window frame was now standing in front of me. I can still see her face in my mind and the warmth of the smile on her face still sends comfort up my spine. She reached her hands to either side of my face, and with big brown eyes widened she said to me in a tone that I can still hear, 'Bella is doing amazing! She is happy, and free, and dancing. She loves you so much.'

My tears stopped flowing, and in a split moment of time, I found myself in my bedroom. It was crowded with all those faceless bodies of energy who had just come inside. My whole room full of them, some of them standing, others sitting on my bed surrounding my two beautiful sleeping daughters. I watched as those that were on the bed, extended an arm from their bodies to touch my daughters on the arms, and the head, projecting love in words like, 'they are so beautiful', and 'what beautiful daughters they are'. These words accompanied by the most beautiful flashes of light within my space, as if the harmony of those words carried the vibrance of their light and energy. Flashes and flashes of the most magical light encompassed my whole room.

The flashes became brighter and brighter and brighter to the point where there were no more shapes, and I found myself once again sitting up in my bed with the dark of night surrounding me. Where I had tasted the tears of sadness on my lips as I fell to sleep earlier, I had emerged from this experience with the tears of joy flowing down my face, and the greatest amount of love and joy expanding in my heart and my chest. I couldn't believe the feeling of joy which was pulsing through my body, as I reached for my phone to check the time.

Our Bella left this world and entered her new realm at 4.14 am on the 7th June 2016.

I woke to this special experience of love and magical joy within me at 4.50 am on the 7th June 2017.

How frustrating it must have been for her in our physical world to have been held captive in a broken body which limited her expression. I felt the ever-present ease within this moment of her free and powerful, sending angels to our home to give us messages of love, to hold us safely and to let us know that she was doing simply fine with her new-found friends and freedom.

I have gone over this experience many times over the last four and a half years and always come back to a knowing that this was an experience of love. An experience into another realm, which although I don't always understand, happened as clearly as day and night. An awakened state in dream time. One which gave me great comfort at a time when the pain in my heart was so intense, and real and all-encompassing.

The months that followed were held in this experience. A gift to see me through the days where the sorrow I felt tried to take over my experience as I breathed, and worked, and mothered and did my best to live as best I could. Before I slept at night, I would invite another experience such as that one on the 7 June 2017 to bring me comfort. To allow me to feel her in action, to know that she was here with me in spiritual form. I would wish for it so I wouldn't feel so alone.

I was alone. My children were here with me. My friends were by my side supporting me and loving me. But still, I was alone. Grief is a lonely journey when after the initial period of loss, everyone who is so present and forthcoming with support and gifts of time, go back to their own lives and rightly so, they should.

But it's lonely. The Christmas of 2017 I felt that loneliness to my core. Still holding on to the visit of love from that next realm, Christmas time appeared. Believe me, there is no greater time that you feel the loss when those monumental occasions arrive. Christmas. Birthdays. Mother's Day.

Christmas Day of 2017 our shared care arrangements kicked into gear, and that was the Christmas I had my daughters for Christmas Eve and Christmas Morning. I had done my best to keep the Christmas spirit alive, but I know they saw right through it, for they too were feeling the deep hole of missing on that day. After we opened our presents that morning, and their dad came to collect them, I was there. Just there. That's the only way I can really explain it. There, with a Christmas tree, and an empty house. Not wanting to be a burden on anyone in that moment, or for that day, because why should anyone else feel my sadness on this day of joy for so many.

So, I took myself to bed and cried. Just balled really. My parents by this time of 2017, had returned to live once again in Melbourne, and although they had invited me to share Christmas with them in Melbourne that year, my heart could not muster the drive. So, I just lay there cuddled by my doona, aching. Breathing, and aching. Aching and breathing. I hated that Christmas.

Ode to 2016

We started out as friends,
Playing together easily between sunrise and sunset.
We rolled between your seasons,
Winter nights the coldest yet.
We kept our cuddles longer,
To keep your presence from our hearts.
But Winter was the splinter
You left wedged within my heart.

Like a maiden raped and tortured,
Tornados shredded every thread.
Every piece, every line, every thought
Within my head.
I lay bleeding all through Winter
Bewildered and confused.
You continued on your journey
Autumn, your new muse.

With every leaf that fell,
My tears fell gently too.
My broken heart lay dying
The moons cycles whispering to stay true.
With barren branches lifted,
I saw the blessing in this space.
This season made for shedding,

To renew but not replace.
So I gathered all my tears,
And with Spring your newest gift
I watered the barren hollow,
To dissipate the mist.
With each new bud I noticed,
I felt an inner cell renewed.
Slowly my soul found colour
Like blossoming roses bloomed
My eyes removed the dullness
From my bleeding, aching heart,
As the warming coastline held the tide
I felt the ease of Summer in my heart.

The veins of pain replenished,
By the sun's kissing of my skin.
I jumped into your oceans,
I jumped
I jumped
I trusted
Summer's laughter felt within.

I cleansed the remnants of your seasons
With gratitude and tears.
The splinter of your Winter,
Remains the shield against my fears.
I am grateful for your lessons
And I welcome the new day.
You have been my greatest teacher
In every living way.

Disabled Parking

AS I HAVE reflected on previously, grief is both a torrid sea crashing on the shores of perception, and a gentle tide whimsically placing itself within the emotions carried through the day. It shows up when you least expect it and demands to be seen. Sometimes the smallest everyday tasks can hold a memory, a smell, or even a reminder of the journey which is so embedded in the psyche of your mind.

For me personally, grocery shopping is one of those everyday moments which brings reminders of all that is lost and all that is learned.

My girls had returned to me on a Monday following their time with their dads, and we had driven into the Aldi carpark ready for our weekly shopping experience.

It was in the early months of 2018, at a time when I had in my own body, begun to experience some authentic moments of joy, even though the journey of grief still held me.

I scouted my gaze around the carpark to find a suitable spot for us to park, and my heart took a literal pause as I was faced by the disabled parking sign. Two perfectly positioned spaces noticeably wider than the remainder of the parallel spaces held in regimented order. I robotically moved the car into a car space which did not require a permit. We gathered our bags from the back seat and headed towards Aldi. As I walked hand-in-hand with Mahala, the call of my heart drew my eyes towards the two vacant spots with the significant bold symbol. My heartstrings tugged a little harder, as I recalled that special day, almost two years before, when we finally received our beautiful Bella's permit to park in this special spot.

For so long up to that day, inclusion for me meant not worrying about the disabled parking spot, but parking wherever we could. I wasn't concerned with the heaviness of the pram-style wheelchair that held the delicate imprint of Bella's growing body. It never crossed my mind, the significance of extra space on either side of the car, until she became bigger and heavier, and I needed the door to be all the way open to make sure the protrusion of her spine wouldn't catch the frame of the door as I lifted her into my arms. How sweet that resting destination from her seat to my arms was every time. So sweet, as we stood for that moment, both held in painted lines of inclusion and understanding. Her arms wrapped around my neck, her eyes looking deep into mine, with still an extra foot of space from the car, where the wide-open door remained, to the permanent concrete marking of where this sacred space ended. That wider, significant parking spot was part of our memories made, and chipped away a little bit of hardness which had been edged in my muscles from lifting and lifting and lifting.

The build of the wheelchair had two parts to it of course, and even though the weight was more than the weight of her beautiful four-year-old body, I felt great accomplishment at how quickly I could put it together. In that perfectly positioned wider space, with such a significant symbol.

Our shopping experience was always a little more involved when Bella was with us, and how wonderful an involvement that was. Kai pushing the trolley, me pushing the pram, and Bella laughing her head off, as Mahala skipped and danced down the aisle. I am proud to say the skipping and dancing has returned, although it may never completely be as full an experience as it was; yet it's still so full of love.

As we gathered our groceries on that Monday, and made our way back to the car, it was not the tug of my heart which invited me to look once again at the vacant disabled spaces. No. It was the fullness of gratitude which held these spaces in my wide-eyed glance, to acknowledge how lucky we were to have known Bella. To have felt the gratitude in the smallest of pleasures, and the greatest of responsibilities. To have loved, unconditionally, no matter the strain. I am so grateful that for the last year of her life, she was given the BEST parking spot at every location! That beautiful bold symbol represented her struggle and ensured that those who loved her, carried her, held her and believed in her, were provided with more space and less impediment to do it well.

There is no longer a sticker on my window, and Bella's seat no longer fills my rear-view mirror reflection. Although the sadness of this reality has tried to close our hearts in many ways, it is the gentle reminders of her presence that keeps love permanently parked in the empty spaces of our hearts. Her energetic presence, the bold and beautiful symbol, always radiating acceptance, understanding and love.

The provisions of hindsight and reflection which come from grief move through me often. These are the tools I have learned and accepted, which are now embedded in my body, through a deep wanting to heal. To live a full life once again, even though my trusty companion grief stays, and waits, and moves with me through all my moments. Every shopping centre I go to holds a Disabled Parking spot. Every single one. I have found to place gratitude on this perfectly positioned spot holds my sadness safely as I feel the congruence between sorrow and acceptance. It is difficult sometimes, but it is necessary. I have come to understand that grief will never leave, but it is the strength in awareness around my grief that allows the crippling nature of its presence to ease and soften. This awareness for me has been borne from an eventual surrendering into that dark chaotic place, where once existed the flow of love from my heart towards Bella's and hers towards mine. To understand what remains in that space of suffering becomes the teacher of how to rebuild the heart that is shattered. I learn more and more about this experience as I stay curious and humbled by my own suffering.

Therapy of the Mother

I undressed that day
She saw me too
I removed the shield
And the armour too.
She called me in,
To sit a while
To hold her beauty
To linger a while.

She touched my skin
With her breath in breeze,
She helped me open
And we danced with ease.
My wound began to seep,
Rolling down my cheek.
My breath became the beat,
To the kookaburra's melody
Inviting me to weep.

'Rest a while' she bled,
In the sap of stoic soldiers
Guarding my surrender.
As sunlight held strong through the peak,
She reminded me that she too,
Sits in stillness
To soften, to be meek.

Surrender

BEFORE BELLA CAME into my life, I was walking the path of 'normality'. My purpose as a mother and wife my focus. I had created a small yoga studio at our home, and I was slowly establishing a steady client base. Prior to that, and before stepping into marriage and motherhood, I feel that I lived from a place of shallow and ignorant understanding. Life doing me, rather than me doing life for the most part. I was raised in a loving home I believe, under the African sun, in a third world country where fear was just an inbred quality. This fear ingrained from a young age, where the quarrels of a nation impact you on a cellular level, even beyond your own understanding of their impact. Burglar guards on windows, with the anarchy of racial malice the glue that held a country together, almost to the point of not knowing anything else. But I had a good life for the most part. I had a loving mother and stepfather who did the best they could with all that was presented to them. But, in reflection, I see that living in a country which bred alertness, hyper-vigilance and an on-guard mentality most of the time ingrains a sense of danger always being around the corner.

The idea of Surrender was never really something I understood as a child, or even as a young woman. Surrender meant giving up. Giving in. There was almost a weak undertone to the word, and a quality I was never raised with. I was raised to be strong. To survive. To be aware of danger. I went to my first boarding school when I was thirteen. Just a child I was, but I understand why in the country that I lived, this was a blessing. To go to a good school; even if it meant learning to survive mostly on your own. I believe that on a deeper level, I have spent most of my life hyper-vigilant; in defence mode. Always keeping myself safe. How that may have looked on an energetic level, and whatever layers I placed over my soul to achieve that, I did on a subconscious level. The messaging of my youth that was ingrained into my choices and patterns of living are clear to me now. Be safe. Escape. There is danger. These I believe are the patterns of conditioning that have dictated so much of my experience in this life.

Having two healthy children played out beautifully within that conditioning. They met their milestones. They ate solids at the 'right' age, they walked at the expected age, and they continued with this timeline of milestones which you expect from your healthy babies after they enter this world. After Bella was conceived, at the early stage of six weeks pregnant, I began to feel the overwhelm of a deep knowing that something was not right within my body, and this feeling triggered all my conditioning. Be safe. Escape. There is danger. I could feel there was something wrong, but all my natural practices were not able to be engaged with as the fear was in my body, and I could not escape it. The maternal instinct knows. It knows when something is wrong, and it limits your natural way of dealing with that fear. I did not want to have an abortion, even though the pull of energy in my body was telling me that there was something awfully wrong.

I would say that this was my first great lesson in Surrender. I could not stop the looping thoughts in my mind. I would lay on our bed with my hands on my womb to feel into what I was experiencing. My ego mind tried to convince my intuition that it was wrong. That all would be well just like it had been with my two babies previous. But eventually all I could do was surrender to a different way of existing with this fear which was brooding continuously in my body. I began to journal. To write down my feelings around my pregnancy. I felt overwhelmed and fearful. I will never forget one morning I was so called to sit and meditate, to connect to my body to alleviate the need to escape and to feel into what was happening inside. I sat. I breathed. I sat some more. The connection to my breath became stronger, and like the gentle flutter of butterfly wings brushing past my face, I felt the words emerge from my soul, 'Just surrender into it, all will be well'.

This message felt important in our journey, mine and Bella's journey that is. I got up from my meditation and wrote those words down on a piece of paper and stuck them to our fridge. They were my reminder, a message from the depths that I needed to try and surrender to what was happening even though I could feel that there was something amiss, something just wasn't right.

Throughout this journey, the one that extends from the time our Bella was conceived, to the journey that continues following her death, this has been my greatest lesson. To let go of control. To trust that I am safe. To emerge more wholesomely from the need to escape, and to feel into what is occurring, so that I can trust more deeply the power of love and intuition which exists within me. This has been an extremely difficult journey for me, one which I am still learning from and leaning into.

The lessons came more frequently after our Bella arrived. The trust in surrendering to the plan of the Divine, the most powerful universal energy which holds us all in her love. After Bella entered this world, grey and not breathing, all traditions held after birth for me were broken. There was no chest-to-chest connection after she emerged from the birth canal. Rather, her lifeless body was taken to a table next to me to be resuscitated by the team of doctors who stood watching and waiting for her entry into this world. From there she was placed in a hospital crib and removed from the room. My last image of her was the greyness of her skin and the cone shape of her emaciated head. Not the best scenario for surrender as I think back to the bewilderment of how those moments had unfolded. All I could do to maintain some balance was take a shower as Scott went to find out where she was and what was happening.

Interestingly though, my pregnancy with Bella was the first of my three babies where I completely engrossed myself in understanding better birth practices through pre-natal yoga. I studied the practice a few months before finding out I was pregnant with Bella, and so, because the ranting of my mind was so prevalent in the early stages of my pregnancy, I decided to have a birth plan. One which was held within my own spiritual practice. This elevated a sense of empowerment within me, allowing my intuition to shine through more clearly, and to settle my anxious mind around her growing in my belly. When the day arrived that I was to be induced, for the most part of Bella's delivery process, I felt like I had complete control over the experience because I had done the work leading up to that day. The meditative practices held me well through the contractions, helped me to stay in my power in those moments and ride out the wave of painful surges from my body as Bella prepared to enter our world. It was a small window of 'normality' as the labour continued. It was not until the midwife suggested that we may need to have an emergency caesarean as Bella's heart rate was extremely low, that my restless mind took over again. The pain of the contractions became too much, and I eventually had an epidural to hold me through the last part of the labour. Bella's heart rate improved, and my body opened, to bring her into the world.

She emerged grey and lifeless. The placenta which was delivered not long after was grey and held no goodness in its form.

Although in my deepest knowing I understood that something was not right just by the need for resuscitation, I still allowed myself to fantasize with thoughts of 'She will be back soon' and 'We will be going home soon'.

But it was not to be.

All my belief systems around birthing and mothering were broken down from a glimmer of empowerment to nothingness as I waited for further instruction from a power greater than me. Doctors, nurses and midwives. They were my angels at that time. I needed their guidance desperately.

The nurses placed me in a room with another new mum, who was not experiencing the same journey I was. She sat nursing her beautiful new baby as I entered the room. The curtain separating our two hospital beds was open, so that I could see her joy, her love and her perfect little baby with her perfect little head. Bella had been placed in the Neonatal Intensive Care Unit and so I placed my bag down on the floor next to the hospital bed and sat for a while to take in the entrapment I felt, in feelings I didn't completely understand. I decided to escape the cooing of love coming from the other side of the room and made my way to the NICU to be with my baby.

That night, after spending the day looking at and attempting to understand the bright medical light that was placed over my girl, I returned to my room to sleep as my body and heart were confused and vacant, with pain waiting to absorb them both. As I climbed into the sheets of that hospital bed, memories of that exact same positioning of my body from years before after the birth of my daughters Mahala and Kai came rushing back to me. The scenario didn't even in any form match the elated pleasure I felt back then after birthing my babies. I lay my head down on the pillow and unwillingly listened to the gentle suckle of the baby next door to me, enjoying the nurture of her mother's breast. My eyes began to fill with tears, one mixing with the other in the encasing of my right eye, before hitting the pillow.

I could not hold her. I could not sleep next to her. I could not see my Bella at that moment. All that was available to me came instinctively, as I prayed. I sobbed and prayed to the power that I knew existed beyond me and inside of me, even though it felt like I had been abandoned. I visualised all the love in my heart for my baby. It took the form of the most magical light leaving my heart and flowing from my body in the form of a stream. The most beautiful stream of golden light travelling along the length of the corridor in a wave of continuity. This golden light found the door of the ICU, snuck right under it in my mind's eye, and found the crib where my Bella lay. I could see the light circling my girl, encasing her in a cocoon of golden love until I could no longer see the sharp edges of the crib, only the golden cocoon I had envisaged protecting her through the night and beyond, as she would now face one of her greatest battles. As the visualisation unfolded in my mind, beside her seated on a hospital chair was the image of my grandad on my father's side who had passed many years before. He was watching over her, as we both slept.

Bella's first ten days of life were spent in that the Neonatal Intensive Care Unit at Wollongong Hospital. There's a process of progression you see in the Neonatal ICU. Those babies held in the 'worst case' category are placed at one end of the ward, and as they progress and make gains and begin to heal, they are moved towards the opposite end, until finally they leave this line of progression and head home.

Bella was at the end where everything looks dire. Every breath I took was held in uncertainty and confusion for the most part, but also in a deep love and determination that we would get to the other end of that bloody ward and get home! Scott took care of our other children, and I stayed in hospital with our littlest love. Breast feeding proved fruitless, as Bella had a high pallet and could not attach to the breast. I would leave the cooing of my roomies in the morning, and head into the ICU to express the colostrum from my breast in an attempt to pass on some of the goodness from my body to our girl. On her second day of life the midwives suggested we try formula and Bella took to the small amount that she was given, but on the third day she had an adverse reaction to the formula. She stopped breathing; her little lips turning blue before my eyes. This layered my fear, with more fear, but an automated response aligning with that of the nurses saw us trying another formula. Eventually Bella took to it and we were on our way to filling her weak little body with goodness.

Amongst the uncertainty there were pockets of joy. Small pockets of capturing little wins, and the beauty of our littlest love. My beautiful friend Kate came into the hospital in those early days and captured some gorgeous professional photos of our Bella. Photos I will cherish until the day I die. And the little wins, well they shone through in Bella being moved from the 'sun bed' as I liked to call it with the blistering light above her, to a pink hospital gown, a blanket and her own little crib in the ward. She looked so beautiful in that pink gown, and even though she had a permanent oxygen tube in her nose at this point, she would spend moments through the day with her eyes open and in my arms, taking in this new place she had landed. Bella progressed like a champion through those ten days in the NICU, and on day five of our stay, she was allowed to wear her own clothes. The hospital bag I had taken to the hospital on her arrival day now found its place in the unfolding of Bella's early story.

The first day we could give her a bath was another that brought joy. Scott and I did this together. Her skinny little body floated in the love of Scott's big strong hand, as she enjoyed the warm water that encompassed her.

Those were special moments.

On the seventh day, I was told that I had to go home. The private room I had been upgraded to was needed by another mum. I was told I could return whenever I liked to sit with Bella in the NICU. Leaving her in the hospital and returning home was difficult, but the level of care we received at Wollongong Hospital was exceptional. We felt great comfort in the care Bella was receiving. I went home, and returned every morning. The tenth day arrived and I was able to bring her home to be with her family.

Bella came home on the 10th October 2011. Before we left the Neonatal Ward that was her home for the first ten days of life, we said our goodbyes to an awesome team of nurses and care staff who had cared so well for our baby. I carried little Bella in my arms, walking slowly along the corridors of Wollongong Hospital towards the carpark. I remember looking down at our Bella and taking in her petite size, comfortably cocooned in her blanket in my arms with her eyes tightly shut and her head still showing remnants of fluid in its shape. I remember looking at her with the ache of knowing in my heart, that this journey would be different, and perhaps a difficult one.

Bella did not make many sounds, and those she did were muted. She did not have big cries. She was gentle in her expression. I slept very lightly those first few weeks that Bella was home. I would listen for sounds of her breath while she slept in her cot at the end of our bed. I would check her often. Scott would too. This journey was different. Our baby was different. But our love for her was the constant and saw us through those moments of questioning her health.

Whispers

The Sun rose
And whispered through the trees
I promise you this fresh new day
To continue on, to try again
To find the beauty in the moments
And to love
Love all that has come before today
The pain, the joy, the fear, the grief and sadness
For I will rise again tomorrow
This is my promise to you child of the earth
Use this day I give you
To feel all that is true and wholesome for you.

The Great Mother

SURRENDERING TO THE unfolding lessons continued.

Prior to receiving the diagnosis of Bella having 108 genes missing from her 19th chromosome in her first year of life, our paediatrician had eluded to the fact that Bella was showing signs of Cerebral Palsy. Prior to that again, we had had an appointment with Charlie Teo, Neurosurgeon in Sydney who informed us that the nature of Bella's tone and development was caused from permanent damage in her brain, and that there was no operation that could be done to fix the issue. So, once we got to the eventual diagnosis from the geneticist of the unique and rare condition that Bella had, it was a difficult diagnosis to swallow initially. All of my own conditioning was triggered in massive forms. But here is where I see how Bella's diagnosis allowed us to receive more of the great gifts that her love would bring to all of us, whilst she was here.

I recall at 22 weeks pregnant my doctor recommended an amniocentesis be carried out, as there were signs up until that point that Bella wasn't meeting the required size requirements for the stage of pregnancy I was at. I remember being afraid of what an amnio would mean. The doctor explained to me it was the process of injecting a very large needle into the embryo to retract some fluid so tests could be carried out to check for any genetic issues that may be present. I was afraid of the thought of that needle going into my womb, and the impact it would have on Bella. I also didn't quite understand the outcome should there be genetic issues with my baby. My doctor explained that should there be any severe issues, an injection could be given which would induce an abortion of my baby, and I would have to birth her through that process. I recall how calm our doctor was when he expressed these words. The image and impact of such inducing reactions of fear in my body and my mind, considering I had already felt, up to that point, that there were so many differences with this pregnancy compared to my other two girls. We decided to go ahead with the amniocentesis and a couple of weeks later the procedure was performed. I lay back on the bed, taking in the process of the needle being inserted through the layers of my skin, and down into my womb and watched on the screen as the needle point entered the uterus. I felt no pain and kept my focus on that entry point checking for signs of any disruption to my baby inside me. A week or so later, I received a call from a medical professional telling me that the test results had come back, and everything was 'absolutely fine' with our baby. I was in the car with a friend at the time, and although I received those words, the joy that rose in my body was only fleeting. Those words did not match the constant sensations within me which signified an outcome completely opposite to what was received. I see now that this contrast was another invitation to surrender to what was. The fact that Bella would eventually in her time here with us be diagnosed with a condition that had never been recorded in the world, explained why her condition was never picked up within those genetic tests which were performed during pregnancy. A unique and beautiful wander of this world she was, arriving into this world with the invitation to stay in the moments with her, as her life and purpose unfolded.

Bella's condition was teaching us to live in the moment. To appreciate the special moments we had because we did not know what was going to arrive in the next moment of our experience with her. To appreciate the gift of time because that gift is the most precious of all. To make wise decisions around how that time is spent. To love. To find joy. To go on adventures.

So we did. Oh my goodness we had some great adventures, my three children and I. I'm not talking about white water rafting and bungy jumping! I'm talking about making even the smallest little outing the greatest adventure. Visits to Nan Tien Temple. Long drives. Train and bus rides. Adventures to Melbourne and Queensland. Bella and I would pile up the pram with a blanket and a picnic and go for long walks down to the water's edge on my days off whilst her sisters were at school. She loved being in the pram on those walks. Her favourite thing to do as I pushed and she sat front and centre, was to put her little hand and foot out to the side, catch and feel the breeze. She loved our Great Mother's gift of the kiss of her breeze on her skin. When you experience someone experiencing these simple and magical pleasures, you take them on and want to understand the magic of them too! I learnt this so much from her. To feel the kiss of the Great Mother on my skin. To see the beauty in the trees and the colours which held their form. To be grateful for the ability to do so. She was my teacher in all of these lessons, and she was feeling and expressing those lessons in her own experience of living. Bella's heart was so open with love, her connection to these magical gifts was ever present and held, shared and enjoyed.

Our adventures extended to long drives and singing in the car. Although Bella could not physically join in on the singing, she would laugh in the silent, chest heaving way that she did as Kai, Mahala and I belted out our favourite songs. She absorbed that happiness as she sat joyful in her seat. She thrived on our happiness and felt our pain just as much. How open a heart she had, to sense and experience what we were experiencing and within this lesson, she taught us to see the beauty, to feel the beauty in the gift of just being. I would catch her in the rear-view mirror smiling and loving the feeling of us, all together, being happy.

I began to understand this joy and what she was teaching us through her experience. When my children weren't with me, I would find comfort in immersing myself in the freshwater swimming holes provided by our Great Mother. I would honour myself, and my own struggle as Bella's mother, by giving myself time in nature. I would take myself on adventures. Alone, but so not alone because I felt held in the experience of surrendering to the ever-present nurture and guidance of nature. There is healing in this place. There is nurture in this place. To sit amongst the trees, and feel encompassed and held in their green, in their breathing, in their existence.

When Bella was no longer here with me, and when I was facing the challenge of surrendering to this deep well of pain that existed inside me, I did feel the call of the Great Mother and that call was asking me to surrender to her. Slowly she invited me back to her, and to myself.

I began to understand how each expression of Mother Earth is a beautiful mirror of expression that we embody as human beings. Her violent winds, reflect the violence of our own temperaments. The damage caused by those violent winds, reflect the same consequence of our own indiscretions. How her radiant sun and seasons provide growth and nurture, as our own expansive light from the love in our heart, breeds growth and understanding. I began to see more clearly, even though it had been in front of me for more than 30 years, how nature expresses life and death, just as our own experience through life is reflected. What lives shall die. What breathes will eventually stop breathing, for it is how the cycle continues.

I learnt lessons here in the magic of surrender. How, when my own resistance fights what is naturally in place, I hurt so much more. The Great Mother holds me, I know this, and provides me with opportunity for reflection when I find myself in moments of not trusting in the greater picture of this experience. She nurtures me when I am depleted. Honours me with beauty every single day if I choose to see it. And so, I began to surrender, although I am always a student in this process and at times I still struggle with the concept of surrender. I am getting better at it, as I learn to trust that what is within, is also all around me. As my Bella came, loved and taught, she also left to travel on to the next realm of her spiritual journey. As that pain was all encompassing, it also allowed me to see myself if I trusted to go into it. To travel into the deepest forest of my own experience, my own inner journey, and face the truths of who I am, who I was, and who I emerge to be through death and rebirth. What a magical, painful, and exhilarating experience this journey is.

In 2018, my spiritual adventure took me to the magic of New Zealand. It was only a five-day personal retreat to a place I had seen so many images of, and heard so many stories of its beauty. I just wanted to be in it. To sit in it. To experience it. To absorb the energy of colour, and adventure and solitude as well. I booked my flight and landed in Queenstown in January of that year. I could not believe the crispness held in the beauty of this place. Of the perfection in nature's lines, and boldness of her colour. On the day I arrived, I sat down at the wharf and waited to take in the magic of the sunset, as people bustled here and there. I felt completely held, captivated in fact, when I witnessed the changes in colour as Mother Earth painted this movement of beauty with her intent. The next day, I hired a car and drove towards Milford Sound for my next experience of beauty. On the way I spent the night at a humble holding, and once again took in the sunset over the expanse of green that surrounded the air BnB residence I was staying in. I woke the next morning before the sun had emerged from its slumber, and headed to Milford Sound.

Such a beautiful drive it was as I cruised along long roads, lined by green fields, rolling hills and intermittent stunning lakes. The magical landscape continued for an hour or so, before I became engulfed by the most fabulous and tallest mountains I had ever seen. I pulled over to the side of the road to take in the magnificence of the beauty around me. I stepped out of my hire car into a deep stillness, with only the symphony of a gently running stream, and snow-capped mountains so high in their divinity. The pink sky opening the call of new possibilities as I felt, deeply, just how magical it is to be held in the earth's beauty. My heart filled with so much gratitude in that moment. Not only for the majestic nature of the beauty I was held in, but also for the choice I had made for myself. To give myself space and time away. To trust in the healing power of the Earth. To believe that I deserved to heal, and to grow from the experiences that had passed, and from the greatest loss I would ever experience in my lifetime.

I stayed on the side of the road for about 30 minutes, just taking it all in. Reflecting. Honouring. Breathing. My lungs filling with the crispness of that rejuvenating moment.

I pulled myself away from what will, still to this day, be held as one of the most special moments of my life. I headed down to the water's edge where I joined a group sea kayaking adventure. We had a fun and informative young guide who captivated us with stories of the magical wonderland of Milford Sound and as he navigated between giving instructions and direction, he would say to himself in a joyful tone, 'What a great day to be alive!' My god he was right! We got right up close to monstrous waterfalls and spent two hours navigating the waters of this magical place.

With my heart full, my adventure continued and the next day I ticked bungee jumping off my bucket list as I leapt from the platform of Kawarau Gorge Suspension Bridge in Queenstown.

It was my intention to leap out far, spread my arms like a bird, and experience the sensation of weightlessness, as I fell through the air. What an exhilarating experience that was, and once I got out of the boat down the bottom, all I wanted to do was go again! On a deeper level this experience brought trust and safety to the forefront of my own consciousness and allowed me to step into that place to experience those two powerful forces which often inhibit us as human beings navigating through life. The water under the bridge was a turquoise blue, and the trees a softening of green against the water's beauty in coloured reflection. I found so much gratitude in my body, mind and soul in that space I had chosen to be in, to receive the nurture I was needing.

Howling Swoon

Has anyone else felt the moon?
The winds and tides filtering in.
Her pull towards another place,
Another face, another space.
I have felt her brazen light
Baring down upon my skin
And when I sleep at night
She conjures the dreams which
Swirl and play within.

Has anyone else felt the moon?
My heart a disciple to her cyclic discipline.
My fingers inspired to tear at these threads,
And rush to the peak
Of that mountain and speak
Through my illustrious howl,
And howl … and howl … and swoon.

Has anyone else felt the moon?
She will be back again soon.

Love in All its Forms

I FIND THE psychology associated with this experience through grief interesting at times when I am strong in holding awareness around my thoughts and feelings. It's interesting to me where energy travels when it is pushing and pulsing to be seen and heard, from the inside of our bodies, outward. When your heart's broken, the outward expression of energy is often dark and closed, especially when you are engulfed by the sadness. Being engulfed by the sadness of grief I can honestly say, is one of the most painful experiences of living in my own experience. I would take seventeen broken bones at once over that feeling of pain in my body. The breaking of a heart in this capacity is honestly excruciating, and it can cause a drunk sense of disorientation. To feel your feet no longer grounded into the earth, and that all your roots have been lifted. That you are upturned from the soil of nurture that holds you through life, and inside it feels like every single energetic thread, which is holding your soul together, has been severed and your heart is no longer in the shape it once held before.

This place, a dangerous avenue for a soul healing journey, when decisions are based on toxic impulse just to escape the feelings in your body. It took me some time to learn and understand this.

Finding once again that connection to nature was a wonderful step to begin to place my feet more firmly on the ground, as my Bella would have wanted me too. Visualisation practice here was also imperative in giving me some deeper sense of support. Visualising that as I stepped my bare feet on the soil of this earth, my roots began to embed themselves into her soothing coolness and were received by her love. Bella's loss made me understand more clearly why people turn to God. Going back to nature for me was just that. Connecting to my senses was just that. Feeling into my emotions was just that. Holding my experience in the bravery I had begun to feel to do so, was just that. Returning to myself, to heal myself, was the path of moving towards God for me. My impression of God being the continuous flow of Divine energy which exists in all of creation.

I believe in Spirit. In the realms beyond what we can see. I believe in the energy of this universe existing inside and outside of us, and within this magical equation lies the deep connection we have, to all that exists and breathes. I believe in that connection as the healer too. The call from nature invites feeling into the pulse of our Great Mother in the breeze, in the soil, in the leaves that rustle and the birds that sing. We are all part of this wonderful experience of connection. The pulse of energy driving both her and us. That pulse and that energy to me is the Divine which I turn too.

Whenever I feel sad, or lost or lonely, I pray and ask for guidance. Whenever I feel an awesome sense of joy and gratitude for the blessings in my life, I take a moment to thank the Divine for all that I have, and all that I have been blessed with. Whenever I feel that I am experiencing lack and dismay ... yup, you guessed it, I go to her, to the Divine Energy that flourishes all around and within me, and I ask her to hold me safely through that time.

Yes, I found my God, and she is LOVE. Sometimes the lessons which exist within the grander plan of this experience, are difficult to understand, but I am learning more and more to trust in this Love. The unconditional love that I feel when I connect to her and to the great vastness of her presence. That energy is with me always.

Seen

I wore green that day
So you would not see my eyes
And brown shoes to take your attention
From my hair
My lips moved with valour
So you would not see them quiver
I walked tall that day
To not falter in my shadow
I undressed that day
As history's senses mocked in shrill
I unmasked that day
Awaiting sudden thunder
I let go that day
In deeper seeing
I felt home

Endings and New Beginnings

IT'S HUMAN NATURE I believe, to hold onto experiences for safety. Sometimes, even if the experiences are not good for us, we place lots of preconceived notions into their validity, and often suffer as a result. Learning to surrender to the absolute truth that Bella had died, and she was no longer here in the physical was excruciating, but necessary. Surrendering into that well of grief as I have mentioned before was the beginning of the end of deep suffering. I'm still exploring that well I might add, as it is so very deep with love, therefore so full of healing.

The concept of attachment has often arisen for me on this journey. When your heart is broken, you do clutch for a life raft as a survival instinct. I clutched to many life rafts, with the subconscious underlining that somebody would save me, or step up for me. I was supported, loved and held on the journey, but ultimately the saving rests in the soul. I know that was and is my responsibility.

I worked in government for a long time. About 12 years to be precise. A career which began when Mahala was only two, and where, in the bathroom of our office, I did a pregnancy test and found out I was pregnant with Bella. I cried so hard in the confines of that toilet when the test showed those two lines. Pregnant! I did not want to be pregnant again and my impulsive tears were very real in that moment. In retrospect, that was the beginning of another end, and the start of something new in our lives. A whole other perspective on pregnancy, and birth and a way of life with a child who had special needs.

My government career had held me and supported me through a divorce, through the small milestones that Bella reached, and had gifted me with great friendships. These friendships supported me through the many bouts of sickness that Bella experienced, and eventually her death. I stayed working for the NSW Government for another four years after Bella's passing, and it wasn't until 2020 that I decided I needed to make change. The experience of this industry no longer felt right for my path. I no longer felt that I had anything left to contribute, and that in turn, there was no nurture in the environment I was in, and in the work I was doing. It was beginning to impact my health, both mentally and physically.

The time arrived where I could not go another day without an action plan to get out of the environment I was in. With no job secured to move onto, I sat on my bedroom floor contemplating what my body, heart and mind needed, and considered the ever-present clutching in my need for safety, to this government job that provides security for 'all time'. I battled with the decision to throw it in. The need to pull away from it was so strong, that I succumbed and typed up my resignation letter. I left it on my computer desktop to contemplate for a day. I prayed and meditated on it all day; on this decision that was going to take my life in a totally different direction. Especially considering, I had no other job to go to. With every moment that I sat in silence asking the Divine for guidance, all I received was 'trust' from the deepest whispers of my soul. Of course, the anxiety surrounding this decision tried to muffle the sounds of my intuition with fear-based impressions around money and providing for myself and my children. Although it was quite a lengthy battle in my mind, eventually at 4pm that afternoon I pressed SEND on the already prepared email with the attached resignation letter.

The wheels of change began to turn. The thick tractor wheels pulling through the soil of life, sowing the seeds of something new. A great new beginning! I was called in the whispers to trust in the guidance of the Divine, that was taking me in a direction I knew nothing about yet, only that it was freedom. Another ingrained moment towards freedom. Freedom from attachment, freedom from control, surrendering once again into my truth and trusting that the outcome would be the right one for me, and for us as a family.

A few days later I saw a job advertisement for an administration assistant role working in after-death care. Straight away I felt I would be great at that job. The position offered less money, but I felt an instant sense of purpose in this field of death and after-death care. I went through the recruitment process and was eventually offered the position. Within six weeks, I was successful in securing a management role for this wonderful facility. The rest is history, so they say.

There are so many layers to this experience that have not only held me as I find myself working in an industry where my experiences in life, especially losing Bella, has purpose. Where I can lead from a place of understanding and compassion, to provide care and nurture for those who are walking the long journey of grief. I had found my place, and in my own personal reflections, I was able to measure just how much healing had taken place for me on a cellular level by 2020, because two years prior, I do not believe I would have been able to do the work I do, or provide the level of service I feel is imperative in this industry. Two years prior, this role would have revealed just how far I still had to go in my healing.

Some days I feel Bella with me strongly in my heart, as I am faced with so many varying degrees of loss and grief in families that enter our facility. I am required to have difficult conversations with those who are walking the path, that I have walked before them. I have learnt about my resilience, and the very real necessity for maintaining equanimity in this field. It is this level of equanimity which has been the measuring tool for my healing. I am grateful to manage a facility that provides a safe space for those who enter its doors, and to provide care, nurture and understanding for those who are deceased, and the loved ones that they leave behind. I try and remain curious too around my experience working with death. So many endings and so many new beginnings in every day, working in this field. What a beautiful opening from the universe to the divinity of experience, and I am grateful to be of service within it.

As I sit here, considering endings and beginnings, and the courage it takes to embark on something new, I am reminded of the first day that Bella started at pre-school. Such a big day that was, and such an important decision both Scott and I had to make for her. We noticed Bella, at three years old, becoming irritable with her standard seated and lying down positions. With only so many toys we could entertain her with, and only so many adventures we could go on in the realm of life that we were living, we knew she needed more. The family care we received from physiotherapists and speech pathologist was guiding us towards considering finding a school that could support Bella with the care she needed, but still provide her safe and fun interaction with other children her age. A place that she could feel the stimulation of this wonderful next step in her journey.

Accepting that it would not be us who would be with her during the day at school and knowing that we were her greatest supporters, who understood the nuances of her body, and the sounds she made when needing to communicate her needs caused me great anxiety as we navigated the decision we needed to make for her. Would she be treated right? Would she be cared for in the way that she deserved? How would we know if something went wrong? It was an anxious loop that could only be thwarted by action, and so we contacted Sandon Point Children's Centre in Bulli. This was the school that Mahala had attended for her pre-school years. I contacted Merran, the Director, and asked her the question as to whether they would accept Bella into their care a couple of days a week, and what would be required to do so. Merran was so amazing in guiding me through how we could make it happen, and the steps the school would take from a compliance perspective to ensure that any extra legislative requirements were covered. Bella would be their first special needs student attending their warm and welcoming facility. What a wonderful woman, who I will forever feel the greatest amount of gratitude for, in her unwavering love and care for our girl, and the beautiful team who embraced Bella's uniqueness with all their attention. The team at Sandon Point Children's Centre were a monumental rudder in the growth and development of our girl, when it came to experiences, joy and play. Together, both their team and our family grew, as Bella's newest experience taught us more about what was possible when we worked together.

I drove into the carpark of Sandon Point Children's Centre on the first day of Bella's pre-school adventure. Bella was in her car seat at the back, wearing a bright pink t-shirt and blue shorts, with her soft golden hair in a little ponytail on her head. This was a momentous occasion for us. Both of us. All of us. I sat with her, and unable to hold back my tears, I began telling her about all the friends she would make and that I would be back later to pick her up. She just smiled and made those beautiful warm sounds that she did.

I eventually gathered myself and got out of the car. I put the wheelchair pram together and strapped her gently into it.

At the front of the pre-school was a white fence that secured the courtyard where the children played. They were all running around not noticing us, enjoying the sand pit and other fun activities that entertained them. Bella was drawn instantly to the laughter and the joy that radiated from this new space she was entering. Just seeing her intrigue created a sense of comfort in me to know that she felt safe. I guided her down the side entrance and into the facility, where Merran greeted us with so much excitement to see Bella. Of course Bella responded with her magical smile as we entered the room where she would become one with her classmates. The space where her pureed food would sit equally beside the cut sandwich lunches of others. There was no difference here. Just little children's food in that big fridge.

Curiosity had begun to seep into the minds of those little souls playing inside now as they noticed Bella come through the door. They began to eagerly make their way towards us and surrounded her with curiosity in their eyes. Merran gave me a look of security and care and let me know that Bella would be fine, and that she was going to have a beautiful day. I lingered for a while but understood, eventually, that I would need to say goodbye. As I bent down beside her to tell her how much I loved her and that I would be back later to pick her up, she did not cry. She was far too curious and intrigued by all these little people that were surrounding her, and were the same size as her. They began to communicate with her, firstly with their eyes, and then with small words like 'hello' and 'what's your name?' Bella smiled and engaged in her own way, and with her own beautiful tones of expression.

I made my way back to the car and could not hold back the tears. I felt such a great sense of relief for her to be stepping into this next 'beginning' on her adventure.

Merran sent me photos of Bella throughout that first day of school. She knew how difficult it was for me to leave Bella in an unfamiliar environment, in someone else's care. Photos of her sitting up against some big pillows surrounded by her new friends, and other photos showing her sleeping peacefully on her little portable bed that was no different from the other children's portable sleeping arrangements. I understand that a lot of my anxiety stemmed from my own fear that there would be a lack of inclusivity within the experience we were creating for Bella, and that perhaps we wouldn't know that this was occurring, and that we wouldn't be able to keep her safe. Give an anxious mind a little glimmer of a flame, and it'll burn the whole damn house down with worry! But my anxiety was destined to be smothered in this regard, by the nurture and care that Bella received in her entire pre-school experience.

For the months that followed that first day of school, we would pull up in the car park of Sandon Point Children's Centre and the children playing in the courtyard would notice and run to the gate looking through and chanting, 'Bella's Here, Bella's Here'. An absolute rock star she was in this experience with all her friends who absolutely loved her, even though she couldn't say a word from her mouth. She made some 'besties', like others do in school. Special friends that would push her in her pram, and when her walker arrived, they would help her navigate outside. Merran would tell me stories of some of the games the children would play with Bella throughout their time together. Doctors and Patient was one of them and Bella was usually always the patient and would enjoy the curious play out of these little children putting bandages on her arms and checking her temperature. There would be singing, lots of singing, as Bella sat propped up against a wall of comfy cushions with her special friends in a half-circle around her, singing Frozen's 'Let it Go' with big smiles and curious eyes beaming from their faces.

Bella had a very normal pre-school experience with story time and play time and all the various other activities that fill the day of a pre-schooler. She had her own locker where her bag would be placed, and the fabric sleeve with her name on it alongside her school mates' fabric sleeves, where notes would be placed in for parents to read. Sometimes within that sleeve, there would be beautiful reminders of how wonderful this experience was for our girl, and for us as her parents. I recall crying the day she received her first birthday party invitation from one of her classmates. This obviously sparked more of a reaction in me than in her, because Bella at this stage of her development, was none the wiser around the logistics of a birthday invitation; she was just happy to play and be around her beautiful friends. But I felt a sense of relief in that moment for another milestone of acceptance, based upon my own initial fears for my girl. If I am to peel back the layers of that reaction, I can see that the tears were borne from a need to always keep her safe, and a want for her to be accepted into this world as a less-abled individual with a heart of expansive gold. Perhaps some of my own conditioning through life was shining through here too, because as both a child and an adult I had been exposed to the cruelty of the world, and it was an infection I did not want my Bella to experience. Those fears were my projection, because wherever Bella shone her light, it opened into goodness.

That birthday party invitation from one of her friends just re-iterated the necessity to normalise the experience that we were in, with Bella attending school with able-bodied children, because that's what happens when you find your tribe and you hang out. Yes, you get invited to birthday parties! How fabulous.

New beginnings are always just a brave choice away. As I sit within my own experience of change, and new beginnings, I often think about those days when Bella embarked on the journey of making new friends. At three years old, she found her tribe. I'm so grateful she experienced this privilege in the physical world before she left.

In December of 2017 Merran and the wonderful team at Sandon Point Children's Centre invited both Scott and I, along with our children, to a celebration of Bella with the unveiling of Bella's Cottage. Our family attended this gathering to find the most magical and beautiful wooden cottage built in Bella's honour and standing proud and tall in the courtyard where she had played countless times with her friends. Our family enjoyed lunch and craft activities with the little children and staff on this special day of remembrance, and got to experience stories about Bella being read during story time.

I drive past Sandon Point Children Centre often and look over towards the space that is so ingrained in my memories. From my car, I take in the highest point of the pitched roof of Bella's Cottage, that stands in the corner of that special courtyard where she created special memories. This experience doesn't always trigger tears for me, as I understand and accept that those days have passed yet are always held in the love of my heart. I give thanks for the experiences, both good and bad, and I remember how truly blessed Bella was, that before she passed, she had a pre-school experience like any other. She felt the cohesive love and nurture held within the silky net of inclusion and enjoyed friendship and playtime within it. Children are so intuitive and insightful, and I absolutely know that the memories of those special school days stayed within her heart until its final beat. I'm so grateful that although her frail body caused her pain, there was an immense amount of joy in her experience.

Sit With Me

Sit with me friend,
There is no end,
To what can be discovered,
When two minds meet
And greet
The chronicles of the unchartered.

Sit with me lover,
So we may be held in the pulsing
Of our breath
Entwined
In the gaze of our eyes
The depth too pure for words to be spent.

My hand on your heart
Yours on mine
With each beat feeling
Into the melting of time.

Sit with me warrior,
Share the stories of your scars,
And the battles fought and won.
I too have scavenged and bled,
Forging forward on the front line.
Where hell has blazed her fiery breath
Where what was once mine,
No longer is.

Sit with me child.
The simplicity of your wisdom
Nurtures the seed of magic,
You have planted into mine.
Where colour holds excitement
And with joy
We can colour out of the lines.

Sit with me,
Sweet child
I am listening.

Awakening

THE WELL OF grief is vast and deep. There are many tones, and shapes and colours in its fabric. The way it moves holds no symmetry. Its impact in each moment can only be measured against the varying levels of awareness that those in grief have developed. Well, this is the learning that I have received from my own experience. I understand that my grief is not going to suddenly disappear, but will continue to be a guide calling me to feel into and see the pain which has ingrained itself in my psyche. As Mother Nature has slowly called me back to her, the beauty of her presence has, over time, penetrated the deep darkness of that sorrow. Slowly there is colour returning to that space that bore a thick and sticky blackness after my Bella left.

Although her physical presence has been removed from our home and our lives, it was only through complete acceptance of Bella's death that I understood that we are all just visitors here to this realm of experience in the physical world. This acceptance refers to a deep and ingrained cellular level of acceptance, when the reality of loss breeds those tempered moments where you catch your breath, because you realise that you've lost the most important part of your life … yes, an extension of your flesh, your DNA and your blood. An extension of your own energy has been removed from your maternal space! Those moments when you hold yourself with that beating pulse of sorrow moving through you, through every vein, with a calling to surrender to the reality of your own experience.

This surrendering and acceptance bares down deep into the soul, from which can emerge the tune of sweet harmony or a wail of sadness echoing from its depths. The soul's song serenades an opening to the deeper layers of perception that exist beyond the pain and the attachment to what was. At first there is resistance. A resistance of your own mind to see past this pain, and the suffering of holding on to the physical presence and the love that radiated from that being. But resistance is also where more suffering likes to live. To open to the deeper layers of this experience is an invitation, and not always a gentle one, I might add, to uncover more of the soul's truth and purpose.

My journey through grief has called me to stay curious and maintain a deep sense of enquiry into the spiritual nature of my experience in life. Having visitors at my kitchen window in the dead of night through an awakened dream state, was an extremely specific invitation to understand more of why those experiences occurred for me. There was a flow-on in 2019, when encounters with spirit seemed to unfold more and more. I was afraid to surrender, and resistance ensued, but as the rough edges of that resistance began to soften, I was led even further on a journey of spiritual enquiry. I found myself a spiritual mentor whose name is Val, and I began to learn more about the spirit world through mediumship and psychic awareness development. I am so grateful for this act of surrender, as I was able to experience an even deeper level of acceptance around the path of life, and the journey through death. More so, how the spirit moves on to another experience of reality, returning to a realm past this three-dimensional experience we are currently in.

A more holistic and consistent path of healing followed as I began to explore areas where my mind, my body and my spirit are all equally honoured through this journey. In 2020, I found an amazing therapist, and the day that I arrived in her consultation room, I knew that she and I were the perfect fit as therapist and client. She spoke my language. The language of love, resilience, spirit, synchronicity, and surrender. In addition to that, she holds the space so safely in her clinical understanding and guidance. She has been an intrinsic and invaluable presence for my healing. The well of grief is deep and vast and so, as we have journeyed through the pain of Bella's loss on a clinical scale, peeling back the layers of motherhood, womanhood and sisterhood, the journey has also taken me even deeper into childhood trauma and deep core wounds. I have, through her guidance, been able to access that very deep place of suffering that has been layered and layered over many years of not having the correct tools to really dig deep into the marrow of my experience in this life. I am so grateful to have her on my team.

My yoga practice continues. I attempt to remain consistent in my practice, with at least three sessions a week, but allow myself concessions to this schedule to live in a somewhat malleable state, to dance with the experiences of life, rather than allow them to weigh on my mind as much as they used to. When I step onto my yoga mat I feel home. It is a place where I can holistically work on my physical body, my mental and emotional body and my energetic body, and take care of the home in which my spirit resides.

This healing journey has been a rollercoaster ride saturated with many experiences through trial and error, with many failures and lacklustre results along the way. It has been a journey that has tested my resilience and strength, and that of my children too. However, I finally feel that we have reached some level of balance around how we navigate through each day with this deep scar in our reconstructed hearts. We allow those feelings of sorrow to come to the surface when they need to, giving them permission to stay to be seen and felt, and then to witness them gently falling away as we step into the ongoing moments of our life on this earth. For me personally, this is a continuous education into the prospect of non-attachment, but like I said this is ongoing. We are all just souls doing our best within this human experience whilst we are here on this earth.

I would like to think that we are all just visitors here to this place and that there is room to explore and grow, fail and re-emerge more educated and stronger than we were as individuals before. I believe that this experience is constantly inviting us to rise to the challenge of growth, to look deep inside and understand the authentic nature of our souls, each one so unique and powerful. I am also committed to building my ability to maintain a level of awareness, so that I become less and less entangled in the one step forward and two steps back dance when faced with uncomfortable and conflicting moments. Rather than don the cloak of escapism, I am catching myself in those moments as often as I can, to challenge myself to face adversity with more resilience and courage. To allow the magic to occur in this space when I am vulnerable and express my uncertainty around the next step to follow. I have learnt through therapy, self-enquiry and of course a whole bunch of trial and error, that my voice around my grief is valuable, as my love for my child is borne deep from the ancestral vein of experience and time.

Creed of A Hero

She may be small
But she is mighty
Her lips may quiver
But they speak her truth
She may be older
But wise from all encounters
Her roar, nestled
In the tears she cries
Which water her ancestral roots.

Heroes

THE HEROES IN this story bear no resemblance to one another. They stepped forward authentically within their own consciousness and driven by their own choice, providing softening where only a thorny terrain existed. I am compelled to honour the heroes of our story, although no words could really capture how much these heroes did for us in this journey that unfolded.

Perhaps without them, those suicidal fantasies would have consumed my breath, and I would not have been able to experience the last five years with my children, Kai and Mahala. Hindsight is a wonderful tool for reflection, and as I look back, I see each one of my heroes so gallant in their love, and so unique in their delivery.

Loss and grief are the cues from the universe for the heroes to step forward. You know who your heroes are, because they are already by your side in the everyday challenges that life provides. Suddenly a tragedy arrives on your doorstep and chaos is bred from this arrival. The heroes are the angels who come to help you navigate through the experience, even when the experience makes no sense. The heroes bear the cross of text message check-ins and listening as you try to articulate into words, the pain that is congested in your body. They do not try and solve it, but hold a safe space for the untangling to begin. The heroes are the special ones, that sit waiting in the corridor outside the children's ward on the dark night that she left. Just sitting there. Not wanting to disturb your time or crowd the vigil, but letting you know they are there, should you need them.

The heroes are the ones who decided they could not manage the intensity of emotions which you, as the bereaved, were experiencing in those very dark early days and chose to hold their own and walk away. I am grateful for the space that they created for another's love to step in and hold us. Oh, the heroes! They are the poets and the storytellers, who have shared their souls through sonnet and song, on grief and love and loss and healing, and keep you held in the promise that you are not alone in this suffering, for somewhere in the world another survived this suffering too. The heroes share the whisper of love in your ear when you cannot reach your own love to hold your arms strong, because they want to break under the weight of the world that you are carrying.

They are the teachers who provide safe space for your children to express their feelings. They are the therapists, the healers, and the nurses in the Mental Hospital wanting to understand you, so that you can be set free.

The heroes are all those who somehow held the moments when the moments were slipping away and reminded you of your strength and courage, and the parts of you that you couldn't see because the darkness was too great.

The love of the heroes creates a delicate web of connectivity to land within, when the painful surrender into the darkness of grief holds you down in all its stickiness, leaving space for only gasps of breath. But still that beautiful web lets you know that they are close. That they are near. The heroes are forever in my heart. My love is braced and ready to always be returned, as I stand, aligned always to the needs of my hero's.

Mirrors

I looked in the mirror, and there she was.
Layers and layers of woman staring back at me.
The sensual one. The scared one.
The one who dances in the moonlight, and ventures
So deeply through the well of thought at times.
The broken one. The healed one.
The lover of all that speaks creatively.
I looked in the mirror, and there she was.
A small child swimming in the open sea.
The seer and the misfit, staring back at me.

Hope

HOPE. A FOUR-LETTER word describing so many facets of the human experience. It holds so much meaning in how we heal, how we love, how we embark on new challenges and how we embrace our own indiscretions, flaws and troubles. When we lose hope, the world we perceive takes on a dim shade of grey. Hope is the lift in the internal space between the belly and the heart. It's the skip in your step, and the upturn at the corners of your mouth, as you speak with friends and share plans of adventures to come. Hope is where joy can find a home, and where love may eventually nestle.

Losing hope and finding it again is so very possible. Losing hope has been one of the scariest experiences in my journey through grief; knowing that I was unable to just flip a switch and hope would return. Finding hope came in the simple yet sacred moments that followed surrendering to the pain. One such moment was when I experienced a beautiful butterfly sitting on the broken branch of my frangipani tree. It came into my vision when I had, only moments before, considered how absolutely hopeless I was. That was a magical moment! Although the trigger of hope was only small, it planted a seed and created an intention behind my eyes to see more butterflies.

Hope began to generate laughter. Laughter is vibration lifting to the sky. Hope and laughter together, oh my goodness, what a wonderful combination these two are. To know that even in sorrow there is hope of a brighter day around the corner, and laughter is always available to you if you are prepared to surrender to the moments where laughter exists.

My heart no longer holds its usual form, but slowly piecing it back together and learning about myself through the process has generated new ways of existing in this life. My paper mâché-looking heart bares the scars of that learning. I see it in my mind with many cracks and pieces out of alignment, but that visualisation reminds me of how strong that energy of hope is that flows through my body, and has seen me to this place I am now.

The love of my children has been the greatest gift I could have ever received in this life. It is the only love that has broken my heart so many times, yet filled it even more. Being a mother to Kai Mary, Mahala Grace, and Isabella May is my greatest achievement. One that I am extremely grateful for. Being able to hold them in the love of my heart has been one of the greatest healers on this journey.

So now I carry hope with me always. Hope that I'll continue to find joy in the simple things. To take in as many sunrises as I am afforded. To continue to stay curious about both my pain and my happiness. I am grateful for the beat of my pulse that keeps my energy vibrating within this body, until it no longer beats, and my energy will lift back into the expansive love of the Divine Universal Energy that I am one with, and she is one with me.

I know my Bella will be waiting there for me when my purpose here on this earth is fulfilled.

To my beautiful Isabella May. Thank you for your strength. Thank you for your love. Thank you for choosing me to be your Mumma. Until we meet again, I feel you in the breeze and I see you in the stars.

Forever Yours x

Lessons Learnt

I savour the moments more now.
It is as if through the tornado of darkness,
I have awakened to a deeper awareness,
Of the importance of time spent.

I savour the hugs,
I breathe them in.
I would read two stories at bedtime,
instead of one
If that softened their longing within.

I listen more carefully,
Although I thought I had before.
Not to overcompensate
But to embrace the layers beneath their words
Which ached through the raw.

I savour these moments more now,
Each one so simple
So delicate
Layered in a magnitude of significance.

I am grateful for these lessons,
Birthed through love, birthed through pain.
And here we are together my loves,
Learning to live, in love again.

Isabella May Newland

30.09.2011 – 07.06.2016

Dance little one
within the palm of our Great Mother
We love you, always & forever.

www.ingramcontent.com/pod-product-compliance
Lightning Source LLC
Chambersburg PA
CBHW050315010526
44107CB00055B/2258